Christmas Fare

Christmas Fare

Judith Holder
and
Alison Harding

Webb&Bower
EXETER, ENGLAND

The author and publishers are grateful to Susan Mosdell
for permission to reproduce a selection of her cards
from the collection in the
Barum Toy Museum, Barnstaple, Devon.

Published in Great Britain 1981 by
Webb & Bower (Publishers) Limited
33 Southernhay East, Exeter, Devon EX1 1NS

Designed by Peter Wrigley

British Library Cataloguing in Publication Data

Holder, Judith
  Christmas Fare.
    1. Christmas cards
    2. Christmas cookery
    I. Title   II. Harding, Alison
    769.5   NC1866.C5

  ISBN 0-906671-34-5

Typeset in Great Britain by
Keyspools Limited, Golborne, Lancs.

Printed and bound in Hong Kong
by Mandarin Offset International Limited

CONTENTS

INTRODUCTION 6

HOME-CURED BACON AND HAM 8
SPICED YULE LOAF 10
FRUMENTY AND FLUMMERY..................... 12
MINCEMEAT.................................. 14
MINCE PIES AND TARTS 16
CHRISTMAS GOOSE PYE 18
WINES AND LIQUEURS 20
CHRISTMAS EVE WIGS 22
SHORTBREAD 24
CANDIES AND BONBONS........................ 26
GINGERBREADS 28
THE BOAR'S HEAD 30
ROAST GOOSE FOR CHRISTMAS DAY 32
ALDERMAN IN CHAINS 34
PLUMB PORRIDGE 36
PLUM PUDDINGS 38
RICH PLUM CAKES 40
PARTY DISHES 42
SNOW PUDDINGS AND YULE LOGS............... 44
THE GREAT SIR-LOIN 46
MULLED DRINKS 48
HOGMANAY BUN 50
BANNOCKS AND GOD-CAKES 52
HAGGIS AND MUTTON PIES 54
BALMORAL MENU............................. 56
GAME...................................... 58
THE WASSAIL-BOWL 60
TWELFTH CAKE 62

INDEX 64

INTRODUCTION

Christmas — 'the King of the Seasons all' — is traditionally a time of feasting and goodwill. The age-old midwinter festival, bidding farewell to the Old Year and welcoming the New, has over the centuries combined with the Christian message to make this a season during which celebration and charity each play a major part. In particular, hospitality to friend and stranger alike and the exchange of gifts or greetings have long been associated with Christmas, which once extended beyond the 'Twelve Days' to the later feast of Candlemas in early February. Then, according to the poet Herrick, the great Yule Log was extinguished and the decorations taken down:

> *End now the White-loaf and the Pye,*
> *And let all sports with Christmas dye.*

Like the Yule Log itself and other seasonal customs, the preparation of special food and drink and the sending of special cards belong to traditions whose origins may be obscure, and which may have changed according to fashion or circumstance, but which have retained throughout their uniquely festive spirit.

Although the ancient Egyptians and the Romans are known to have sent each other messages and tokens to mark the New Year, the greetings card as we know it did not appear until comparatively recently. In nineteenth-century England it developed in part from the popular, usually elaborate, Valentine card and also from the less common Christmas or New Year letter which often had a simple appropriate decoration. Thanks to the introduction of the Penny Post in 1840 and the increasing sophistication of colour-printing techniques, the Christmas card rapidly achieved popularity after its first appearance in the early 1840s. Soon the familiar robins, holly and Father Christmases, the glittering 'snow' and gilded lettering became part of the Christmas scene, although for some time the Victorian passion for 'flowers with everything' dominated card design, as it did so much else during the period. Perhaps surprisingly for an era noted for its conventional piety the proportion of 'religious' cards seems comparatively low; rather more emphasis was placed, as the cards themselves demonstrate, upon the good behaviour of children and the charitable deeds of their elders at Christmas-time.

It is, however, to the Victorians that we owe the revival of the 'Old English' Yuletide. Inspired by the example of the Queen herself and by the introduction to England by Prince Albert of the decorated fir-tree and the legend of St Nicholas, the nation became wholeheartedly devoted to the ideal of the family Christmas. Turkey, roast beef and plum pudding, mince pies and rich fruit cake were taken for granted, but there was a renewed interest in the ancient customs and dishes of the past. Thanks to the Puritans, two centuries earlier, much of the merry-making and lavish feasting had declined; though huge Christmas pies, mincemeat and spicy Yule breads continued to be made, the roasted swans, and gilded peacocks and the great 'marchpane' cakes of

MAY CHRISTMAS ALWAYS BE TO THEE, A TIME OF MIRTH AND JOLLITY ·

"The Turkeys, Madam, you see here, are tender, plump, and far from dear"

THE COMPLIMENTS OF THE SEASON, AND ALL GOOD THINGS IN REASO[N]

They're doomed for Christmas brawn and chine for pigs must die that men ma[y]

Elizabethan times had long since vanished. In the nineteenth century, however, plumb porridge and the boar's head were immortalized in the poems of Sir Walter Scott, whilst the wassail-bowl appeared in fashionable houses as well as in the countryside where it had originated. Anthologies of Christmas verse and the appearance of Charles Dickens's Christmas tales not only added to the general sentiment but also influenced the design of cards.

The Victorian and Edwardian cards which illustrate this book have been chosen for their intrinsic charm and interest, as well as for their evocation of the traditional festive atmosphere. Many of the recipes which accompany them are to be found in cookery books of the eighteenth and nineteenth centuries. Others are regional or family specialities which have survived the changing fashions in diet and cookery and provide links with popular customs that few can now remember. The 'Old English Christmas Carol' which follows appeared in 1873 on one of the most popular cards of the decade: it reflects both the romantic nostalgia and the practical goodwill which were part of the old-fashioned celebration of Christmas.

This popular four-fold card by the famous publishing firm of Marcus Ward appeared first in 1873. Although it was possible to buy each card separately, the four were often, as in this well-preserved example, enclosed together in decorative wrappers printed with verses appropriate to the 'mediaeval' theme. The detailed drawing and delicate colours, together with the quotation above and below each picture, place these small cards at the forefront of Victorian Christmas card design.

Now that the time is come wherein
   Our Saviour Christ was born,
The larders full of beef and pork,
   And garners filled with corn;

As God has plenty to thee sent,
   Take comfort of thy labours,
And let it never thee repent
   To feast thy needy neighbours.

Let fires in every chimney be,
   That people they may warm them;
Tables with dishes covered,
   Good victuals will not harm them.

With mutton, veal, beef, pig and pork,
   Well furnish every board—
Plum-pudding, furmity, and what
   Thy stock will then afford.

No niggard of the liquor be,
   Let it go round thy table;
People may freely drink, but not
   So long as they are able.

Good customs they may be abused,
   Which makes rich men so slack us,
This feast is to relieve the poor,
   And not to drunken Bacchus.

Thus if thou dost, 'twill credit raise thee,
God will thee bless, and neighbours praise thee.

MAY CHRISTMAS BRING THEE PEACE AND PLENTY, BARNS & CELLARS NEVER EMPTY

"A horn of honest wholesome beer will warm the heart—the spirits cheer."

MAY GOOD DIGESTION WAIT ON APPETITE, AND HEALTH ON BOTH

"Wife, husband, children on their way to dine with friends on Christmas day."

HOME-CURED BACON AND HAM

For families in many parts of the English countryside Christmas began in the late autumn with the killing of a pig. This was in itself a festive occasion as well as a time for hard work: the results were seen in well-cured hams, pork pies, sausages and sides of bacon which lasted till Christmas of the following year. Home-baked pies were often sent as gifts and no Victorian party was complete without the decorated ham which graced the sideboard or dinner-table. The famous cook Alexis Soyer described ham as a 'useful and popular dish, equally a favourite in the cottage and the palace'.

Curing was a lengthy business. First the joints were carefully rubbed all over with a mixture of salt, saltpetre and sugar, then left in large earthenware ham-pots for a few days. Next a brine or pickle was poured over them and the hams were steeped for several weeks, being turned and basted every two or three days. Different types of ham required different ingredients; the special flavour of Suffolk sweet-cured hams came from the mixture of treacle, brown sugar and hot stout in which they were soaked, and it was thought that Yorkshire hams were superior on account of the high quality of the local salt. For smoking, the final stage, wood ash was considered essential. Smoking was done either in the chimney at home or in a local smoking-house and took several more weeks, after which the hams could be stored in straw or ashes until needed.

According to Mrs Rundell's *Modern Domestic Cookery,* 'It is an invariable practice to serve salt meat of some kind with roast turkey; either ham, tongue, bacon or salt chine; the latter principally at Christmas.' For such a special event a ham would often be baked after thorough soaking to remove all salt. Eliza Acton gives the following instructions.

Lay it with the rind downwards into a large common pie-dish; press an oiled paper closely over it, and then fasten securely to the edge of the dish a thick cover of coarse paste. Or, lay the ham on the paste, of which sufficient should be made and rolled off to an inch in thickness, to completely envelope it. Press a sheet of oiled paper upon it; gather up the paste firmly all round, draw and pinch the edges together, and fold them over on the upper side of the ham, taking care to close them so that no gravy can escape. Send it to a well-heated, but not a fierce oven. A very small ham will require quite three hours baking and a large one five. The crust and the skin must be removed while it is hot.

The simple flour-and-water paste, which today can be replaced by a covering of foil, was discarded along with the skin. This method, preserved the flavour and juices of the meat and was also used for baking a haunch of venison or the popular salt bacon chine. A chine—part of the pig's backbone—would first be soaked, then scored into the bone and the cuts stuffed with sweet herbs or parsley-and-thyme forcemeat; it was then baked as above or roasted slowly. Mrs Rundell suggests serving it with a mushroom sauce rather than the usual apple sauce. A chine which was to be served cold would be stuffed, tied up in a bag or cloth and boiled for several hours. Some cooks also preferred to parboil a ham before baking or roasting: one way of making it more succulent was to boil it with a piece of beef and some lean vegetables, which afterwards made a splendid broth for the family.

When cooked, a ham was either served hot, sprinkled with raspings of bread and chopped parsley, or allowed to cool in its liquor before being glazed and decorated. The aspic jelly so often used for decoration was in fact a very stiff tarragon-flavoured consommé, which had the disadvantage of becoming stale much sooner than the ham itself. Elaborate ornamentation, therefore, was really only feasible for more well-to-do families, and most people made do with the conventional paper frill and bunch of parsley, or perhaps some 'flowers' of cut carrot or fried bread. Mrs Acton states that 'in general, English cooks had less skill in decoration than Continental ones'; but it is in an English recipe book, *Dolby's Cook's Dictionary* of 1830, that we find instructions for making a 'Ham in March-pane'.

Clearly intended as the centre-piece of a feast, this was made from nine pounds of almond paste, coloured red, with 'thin pieces of white paste inserted to represent the veins of fat in the lean'. The ham shape was covered with a 'skin' of white marzipan, then with chocolate to imitate the glazed rind; finally it was sprinkled with 'crushed macaroons to resemble the rasped bread with which a boiled ham is generally covered'. Not surprisingly, this is a recipe which seems to have disappeared from later Victorian cookery books. However it serves as a reminder not only of a more lavish age but of those cooks whose artistry more than made up for their lack of modern equipment.

Compliments of the Season

Among the earliest Christmas cards are those which developed from
the conventional visiting-card. From about the middle of the nineteenth
century special designs were printed in gay colours, on small cards,
which were increasingly used to convey seasonal greetings to
friends and relations. Two favourite themes — feeding the birds
and decorating the home with traditional holly — are used on
these cards with a freshness and clarity characteristic of
earlier designs, acting as pleasant reminders of
the simple country Christmas.

A merry christmas

SPICED YULE LOAF

In parts of Yorkshire and Lancashire it is still the custom to bake special fruit loaves well in time to offer to pre-Christmas visitors or send as gifts to friends and neighbours. Earlier recipes use yeast, the cakes being set to rise like bread, while later versions use baking-powder instead and perhaps wine for mixing rather than milk. Usually these loaves are made in addition to the richer Christmas cake; the latter is generally iced and decorated, whereas spiced bread or cake is left plain and served with cheese in the traditional way. Here is a Yorkshire recipe for a simple currant loaf which is made a little more festive by the addition of candied peel.

Sieve four pounds of flour with half an ounce of salt, then rub in one pound of lard and twelve ounces of good butter. Mix a quarter of a pint of fresh brewer's yeast in one pint of warm water, then pour into a well in the centre of the flour. Mix and rise in a warm place, as for bread. When risen knead in three pounds of currants, a pound and a half of soft brown sugar, grated nutmeg or mixed spice to taste, and four ounces of chopped candied peel if

liked. Lastly add four well-beaten eggs, very gradually, and mix the whole thoroughly. Half fill greased loaf tins with the mixture, prove, then bake in a hot oven for about forty minutes.

Another North of England recipe uses black treacle and wine for a really dark mixture which can be baked in either one large loaf tin or two medium-sized tins.

Cream together half a pound of butter, half a pound of brown sugar, and half a pound of black treacle. Add four well-beaten eggs and a large glass of sweet wine; mix well. Add ten ounces of flour, already sieved together with two teaspoonsful of baking-powder and one of mixed spice; lastly add twelve ounces of washed and dried currants. Line the tins with paper, put in the mixture, and bake for about two hours in a fairly slow oven.

Most recipes for Yule bread seem to have been either handed down from one generation to the next or included in hand-written cookery books, and there are of course local variations. In Scotland the loaves are still made with yeast and enriched with plenty of

Produced by the firm of Joseph Mansell, one of the foremost publishers of greetings cards in the mid-nineteenth century, this charming small card has as its base a visiting-card printed with a wintry countryside scene. The cut-out designs of solemn-looking little girls and a Christmas fir-tree are fixed on with paper hinges, enabling them to stand away from the background, whilst a tiny cut-out robin is glued on to the foreground.

fruit and chopped almonds. The following old-fashioned recipe comes from Cornwall; it uses honey and raisins and was at one time eaten with cheese as part of breakfast on Christmas morning.

> Sieve a pound of flour with a pinch of salt into a warm basin, then add half an ounce of fresh yeast, previously dissolved in a cupful of warm water. Mix and set to rise, the bowl covered with a cloth. When risen, add half a pound of creamed butter, together with three tablespoons of honey, six ounces of sugar, twelve ounces of currants or raisins, four ounces of chopped peel, and two well-beaten eggs. Add also one teaspoon of mixed ground spice, and work all the ingredients together until the mixture is smooth. Put into two warm, greased loaf tins, prove, then bake in a moderate oven for about one and a half hours.

Yet another variation appeared under the heading of 'Yorkshire Spice Cakes' in a crudely-printed but evidently popular collection of Edwardian *Prize Recipes*. The compiler of this booklet obviously expected readers to be catering for a very large household or a considerable number of Christmas visitors; the ingredients given here, however, could be halved to meet more modest modern needs.

> 7lb flour, 6oz baking powder, 5lb currants, 2lb stoned raisins, 2lb demerara sugar, 1lb candied peel, 4 grated nutmegs, 12 eggs, 1½lb butter, 4 pints milk.
> Mix flour with baking powder. Rub in butter, nutmeg and all other dry ingredients, and, lastly, add eggs well beaten with the milk, and bake in a quartern square tin for one and a half hours. This is made in Yorkshire for Christmas, and if kept in a good deep bread pan, well covered, will keep three or four months, and improves with keeping.

These loaves are more like our present-day Christmas cake than true currant bread and could be made either in loaf tins or round cake tins instead of the 'quartern square tin' suggested in this recipe. According to a cookery notebook written in the early nineteen-hundreds, a good way of keeping fruit loaves or cakes fresh was to 'wrap them in clean old napkins dipped in grape juice or cider and wrung nearly dry'—a method which no doubt added to the rich spicy flavour when they came to be eaten with cheese and home-brewed wine or beer.

This card, made from paper-lace foundation with 'scrap' picture and ivy wreath fixed on to it, clearly has its origins in the popular valentines of early Victorian times. Special Christmas scraps, particularly those featuring robins, came to be widely used, both for home-made and factory-produced Christmas cards, until superseded by the more sophisticated printing techniques and mass production of the later nineteenth century.

FRUMENTY AND FLUMMERY

Frumenty is a spicy concoction still remembered as a kind of wassail cup in counties as far apart as Yorkshire and Somerset. It was often made at harvest-time in the country but was also served to carol-singers on Christmas Eve, along with spice cakes and cheese, and mince pies. A recipe from *The Healthful Cookery Book* of 1812 states that 'frumenty is made throughout the county of Durham at the Christmas festival as an indulgence to children', and in its simpler form as a porridge or gruel it was certainly more suitable for children or invalids than for adult festivities. Originally 'made from new wheat beaten in a stone mortar until the husk is loosened', like many other unsophisticated dishes it became richer and more elaborate in Victorian times. By 1853, according to Mrs Rundell's *Modern Domestic Cookery*, 'Somersetshire Frumenty' has egg yolks and nutmeg added as well as a liberal dash of rum or brandy. The 'furmety tent' at country fairs was regarded by the righteous as a source of wickedness and immorality on account of the alcoholic additions which made frumenty so potent, thus causing the downfall of working men like Michael Henchard in Thomas Hardy's *Mayor of Casterbridge*. Here is a modern version of the dish.

> Take a large cup (about eight ounces) of wheat or barley 'pearls', and place with a pinch of salt and a quart of water or skimmed milk in a covered casserole or heavy saucepan. Simmer very gently and slowly either in a slow oven or over low heat for several hours, until all the liquid is absorbed and a soft 'cree' forms. Stir from time to time, if necessary adding more liquid, then remove the pan or casserole, and strain off any surplus liquid. Then add a quart of heated, fresh milk, and stir in raisins or currants, sugar and grated nutmeg to taste. Cook gently for about an hour longer, then cool and thicken the mixture with either a little cornflour or two beaten eggs. Add brandy or rum, and serve either hot or cold in a large bowl, with cream if you wish. If only a small quantity is needed, take only two or three spoonfuls of the 'cree' and add about half a pint of milk, with sugar, fruit and spices to taste; the remainder will keep fresh for several days.

In mediaeval times frumenty was a solid mixture which could be sliced like cake. Later, however, it was widely used as a drink or gruel like the Scottish 'sowans'. This was made from the inner husks of oats after threshing. The husks were soaked, sometimes for weeks, and the resulting liquor drunk or used to make scones whilst the sediment made a kind of porridge which could be served with milk or cream.

Like frumenty, sowans would, on special occasions, be well-laced—with good Scotch whisky of course. According to Marian McNeill, an authority on Scottish cooking, Christmas Eve was until quite recently known as 'Sowans-nicht' in some parts of Scotland. *The Healthful Cookery Book,* however, places a recipe for 'Flummery or sowins' firmly in the section on 'Diet drinks for the sick'; coarse oatmeal is used and it is in fact a plain oatmeal porridge. Later in the century Mrs Rundell gives a more interesting version.

> Put three large handfuls of very small white oatmeal to steep a day and a night in cold water; then pour it off clear and add as much more water, and let it stand the same time. Strain it through a fine hair sieve, and boil it till it be as thick as hasty pudding, stirring it well all the time. When first strained, put to it one large spoonful of white sugar and two of orange-flower water. Pour it into shallow dishes, and serve to eat with wine, cider, milk, or cream and sugar. It is very good.

Other kinds of flummery were made with cream stiffened with ground rice, isinglass or hartshorn jelly, and these were often decorated with candied fruits or blanched almonds. A really stiff mixture could be used in a mould for a specially decorative dish, like the following 'Temple' in flummery which appears in Richard Dolby's *Cook's Dictionary*.

> Divide a quart of stiff flummery into three parts, colour one part pink with a little bruised cochineal, steeped in French brandy. Scrape an ounce of chocolate, dissolve it in a little strong coffee, and mix it with another part of the flummery, which will make it a stone colour, and have the last part white; then wet the temple mould, and fit it in a pot to make it stand even. Fill the bottom of the temple with pink flummery for the steps, the four points with white, and fill the rest up with the chocolate flummery, and let it stand till the next day; then loosen it very gently from the mould, and turn it out. Stick sprigs of flowers from the top of every point, which will strengthen it, and give it a neat appearance. Lay round it rock candy sweetmeats for garnish.

Such recipes as this, and the illustrations of elaborate moulded desserts and party dishes which appeared in some popular cookery books, show how much could be achieved even without the patent jelly and blancmange mixtures of later times.

This beautifully preserved card reflects the care
so often lavished upon these small objects, especially
towards the end of the Victorian era. The girl's picture,
printed in delicate colours on white satin, is framed by a
heavily gilded, embossed design. The tiny flowers
at the scalloped edges are sewn with pink silk and
there may also have been a silk tassel attached
to the bottom of the card.

Children were popular subjects on early cards
and the Victorians were always ready to point out some kind of moral
to the young. The message on this boy's book reads,
FOR A GOOD BOY,
.and he certainly looks angelic enough to receive plenty
of Christmas rewards. The card is a typical production of the
London firm of Sulman, noted in the 1860s for their elaborate
little cards. Many of them, like this one, had decorative
edges and embossed patterns with the centre left blank
for the addition of a coloured scrap.

MINCEMEAT

This is one of the oldest Christmas delicacies and one of the richest. The many spices used were once thought to represent the gifts of the Kings, but in fact were important, along with the brandy or wine, to help preserve the meat which was originally an essential ingredient. Many recipes used beef, either boiled or roasted; according to the author of *The Cook's Oracle* of 1823 tripe or the yolks of hard-boiled eggs were sometimes substituted for meat, but 'the lean side of a Buttock of beef, thoroughly roasted, is generally chosen', as in this recipe from the same book.

Two pounds of Beef Suet, picked and chopped fine; two pounds of Apple, pared and chopped fine; three pounds of Currants, washed and picked; one pound of Raisins, stoned and chopped fine; one pound of good Moist Sugar; half a pound of Citron cut into thin slices; one pound of Candied Lemon and Orange Peel, cut as ditto; two pounds of ready dressed Roast Beef; free from skin and gristle, and chopped fine; two Nutmegs, grated; one ounce of Salt; one of ground Ginger; half an ounce of Coriander Seeds; half an ounce of Allspice; half an ounce of Cloves; all ground fine; the juice of six Lemons, and their rinds grated; half a pint of Brandy, and a pint of sweet Wine. Mix the Suet, Apples, Currants, Meat, Raisins and Sweetmeats well together in a large pan, and strew in the Spice by degrees; mix the Sugar, Lemon Juice, Wine and Brandy, and pour it to the other ingredients, and stir it well together—set it by in close-covered pans in a cold place; when wanted, stir it up from the bottom, and add half a glass of Brandy to the quantity you want.

At about the same date the author of a famous Scottish recipe book (written under the pseudonym of Meg Dods) remarked rather cynically that 'every family receipt-book teems with prescriptions' for mincemeat. Her own preference was to use a neat's, or bullock's, tongue; this involved rubbing it with salt and spices and leaving it for three days before boiling and then mincing it—an indication of the time-consuming preparations often lavished on such specialities as mincemeat. Perhaps wisely Mrs Dods also suggests that gravy may be used instead of wine for a cheaper dish, and many cooks already preferred to make it without meat.

Later in the century Mrs Rundell gives her recipe, which still tastes good, even if made with smaller quantities of port and brandy than she recommends.

Of the best apples six pounds, pared, cored and minced; of fresh suet, and raisins stoned, each three pounds, likewise minced; to these add of mace and cinnamon a quarter of an ounce each, and eight cloves, in finest powder, three pounds of the finest powder sugar, three-quarters of an ounce of salt, the rinds of four and juice of two lemons, half a pint of port, the same of brandy. Mix well and put into a deep pan. Have ready washed and dried four pounds of currants, and add as you make the pies, with candied fruit.

The practice of adding some ingredients just before baking seems to have been a common one and perhaps goes back to the times when all the meat, fruit, spices and sweetmeats were placed in layers, usually beneath one large crust rather than in a number of smaller patties.

Special Christmas postcards rapidly became popular after the introduction of the common postcard in 1870. The children on these turn-of-the-century cards are clearly enjoying the more sophisticated pleasures of Christmas in town among well-to-do

14

Generally the Victorians seem to have made large quantities of mincemeat, often several weeks or even months before Christmas. One widely recommended method of keeping it fresh was to store it in small jars, covered with circles of plain paper dipped in brandy, and tied down well. There were times, however, when a special recipe made for just one occasion called for smaller amounts, as in the following for 'Lemon Mincemeat', again taken from Mrs Rundell.

Squeeze a large lemon, boil the outside till tender enough to beat to a mash, add to it three large apples chopped and four ounces of suet, half a pound of currants, four ounces of sugar; put in the juice of the lemon and candied fruit as for the other pies. Make a short crust, and fill the pattypans as usual.

The instructions for 'Egg Mince Pies' are similarly quite simple; these were known also as 'Lent Pies', having no meat and little alcohol.

Boil six eggs hard, shred them small; shred double the quantity of suet: then put currants washed and picked one pound or more, if the eggs were large; the peel of one lemon shred very fine, and the juice, six spoonfuls of sweet wine, mace, nutmeg, sugar to taste, a very little salt, candied orange, lemon, and citron. Mix together and make a light paste for them.

households. Mistletoe and holly garlands, candle-lit trees and exciting presents; all were part of the romanticized version of the festivities as reflected in the increasingly commercialized greetings cards. Many people, including the editors of Punch, disapproved, but there is now a special charm about these designs – often heavily gilded or on gold or silver card, and their seasonal messages more prominent than on the simpler, earlier cards.

MINCE PIES AND TARTS

It is hard to believe that the familiar mince pie was once banned by the strict Puritans of the seventeenth century. Chiefly they disapproved of the popular idea that the pie-crust, then oval or boat-shaped and called a 'coffin', represented the cradle of the infant Christ. But the ban also extended to rich ingredients and alcohol in general which by then were firmly established as part of the feasting and merry-making associated with Christmas. After the Restoration, however, the festivities were made legal again and since then mince pies have regularly appeared in the shop windows of pastry-cooks during the Christmas season.

Here is a recipe for the puff paste of which they were usually made. Most cookery books made recommendations as to the coolness of the room where the puff paste was mixed, and some stated that it should not be made after daybreak; this recipe, however, has the added authority of Thomas Shoesmith, compiler of *The Biscuit-Baker's and Pastry-Cook's Assistant*. His method is surprisingly simple.

> Take one pound of flour, and eight ounces of butter; rub the butter into the flour with your hand, and make it into paste with water, to the consistency of very thick batter; roll out your paste thin, break eight ounces more butter into pieces the size of a shilling, and put them in all parts of the paste: fold it up, and after standing a short time, roll it out again: when it has been rolled out three times, it is fit for use. . . Roll your puff-paste in sheets; cut out the tops to the size of your patties, about as thick as a penny-piece; put your cuttings for bottoms; fill them as to your fancy, cover and close them, and bake them in a steady oven.

Mince pies were often removed from the oven when nearly baked and given a sugar glaze or icing made by brushing them with whisked egg-white and sifting fine sugar over them. A few drops of water were then sprinkled over and the pies were returned to the oven until baked a delicate golden-brown.

Eliza Acton in her recipe for 'Mince Pies Royal' suggests a meringue covering for the pies, to replace the usual pastry lid. Caster sugar can be used here instead of 'pounded sugar'.

> Add to half a pound of good mincemeat an ounce and a half of pounded sugar, the grated rind and the strained juice of a large lemon, one ounce of clarified butter, and the yolks of four eggs: beat these well together, and half fill, or rather more, with the mixture some patty-tins lined with fine paste; put them into a moderate oven, and when the insides are just set, ice them thickly with the whites of the eggs beaten to snow, and mixed quickly at the

moment with four heaped tablespoonsfuls of pounded sugar; set them immediately into the oven again, and bake them slowly of a fine light brown.

Another Victorian speciality was the 'tourte'. For this, puff pastry was made using four ounces of butter and eight of flour and rolled out three-quarters of an inch thick. It was cut with a large round fluted cutter and the shape laid on a floured tin. With a much smaller cutter rounds were cut from the remaining pastry, rolled out about a quarter of an inch thick. The small rounds were overlapped and pressed round the edge of the larger circle in which an incision was then made with a knife point, all round the inside edge of the border, cut not too deep or too near the smaller circles. When the pastry was sufficiently baked in a gentle oven it was cooled a little and the centre part of the crust carefully removed. It could then be used like a vol-au-vent, either with a sweet or savoury filling. Eliza Acton gives the following instructions for 'Christmas Tourte à la Chatelaine'.

> Make the case for the tourte, and put sufficient mincemeat to fill it handsomely into a jar, cover it very securely with paste, or with two or three folds of thick paper, and bake it gently for half an hour or longer should the currants, raisins, etc not be fully tender. Take out the inside of the tourte, heap the hot mincemeat in it, pour a little fresh brandy over; just touch it with a strip of lighted writing-paper at the door of the dining-room, and serve it in a blaze; or if better liked so, serve it very hot without the brandy, and with Devonshire cream as an accompaniment.

The Victorians seem to have loved spectacular dishes of this kind and often ordinary mince pies were served, like this more elaborate tart, in a blaze of rum or brandy.

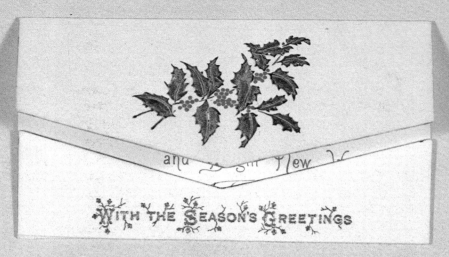

WITH THE SEASON'S GREETINGS

*Holly and mistletoe have been part of the winter festival
since pre-Christian times; like the mince pie they have a long history
and certainly the Victorians used them, along with the robin,
on even the earliest cards. These cards also reflect, however,
the importance of the Penny Post and of envelopes, both of
which played a large part in the development of the Christmas card.
Many were made, like the one shown here, to open like a
small envelope with the sender's greeting and name inside,
while on the unusual 'pillar-box' card, dated 1878, the door opens
to reveal one greeting on the back and another printed on
a tiny folded piece of paper.*

CHRISTMAS GOOSE PYE

In spite of the fashion for 'healthful diet' which influenced much early Victorian cookery, the traditional English 'great pye' continued to be popular. It was, however, becoming modified to suit the demands of an age which, though often seeming by present-day standards to have eaten excessively, was in fact less wildly extravagant than preceding centuries. The recipe for a 'Yorkshire Christmas Pye' given by the famous eighteenth-century cook Hannah Glasse included 'a turkey, a goose, a fowl, a partridge and a pigeon'; these were placed one inside the other and then flanked with a hare on one side and woodcocks and other wildfowl on the other. All these were baked within a 'standing crust' which took a bushel of flour, and readers were advised that 'these pies are often sent to London in a box as presents, therefore the wall must be well built'.

Mrs Glasse's recipe for a 'Goose Pye' is rather more modest, however. It appears again, almost verbatim, as 'A Christmas Goose-Pie' in *The Cook and Housewife's Manual* fifty years on in the 1820s.

> Bone and season highly a goose and a large fowl. Stuff the latter with forcemeat made of minced tongue or ham, minced veal, parsley, suet, pepper and salt, with two eggs. Stew them for twenty minutes in a little good broth in a close stew-pan. Put the fowl within the goose, and place that in a raised pie-crust, filling up the vacancies with forcemeat or par-boiled tongue or pigeons, partridges, etc. Put plenty of butter over the meat. This pie will take three hours to bake. It will eat well cold, and keep a long while.

The author, Meg Dods, adds the note that 'this receipt still keeps its place in cookery-books, though the pie itself is now as rare as the capercailzie or the wild boar'. Yet, years later still, it reappeared in Mrs Rundell's *Modern Domestic Cookery* with the additional instruction to 'ornament the top and let it be moveable, so that the pie may have a good appearance to the last, as the crust is not to be eaten'. She also suggests seasoning the birds well 'with pepper, taking care to cover the whole of the interior, or otherwise it will turn sour before it can be eaten'— a wise precaution, since the pie would be made before Christmas and was expected to last well into the New Year.

Clearly the ancient art of pie-making was still very much alive. As Mrs Rundell explains, 'Raised Pies may be made of any kind of flesh, fish, fruit or poultry, if baked in a wall of paste instead of a baking-dish; but they are generally eaten cold, and made so large and savoury as to remain a long time before being consumed, for which reason they also bear the name of "standing pies".' She then gives instructions for making the hot-water crust for raised pies.

> Boil water with a little fine lard, and an equal quantity of fresh dripping, or of butter, in the proportion of 2oz. of fat to 1 pint of water. While hot, mix this with as much flour as you will want, making the paste as stiff as you can to be smooth, which it will become by good kneading and beating it with the rolling pin. When quite smooth put a lump into a cloth, or under a pan, to soak till nearly cold... The proper way to raise the crust is by placing the left hand on the lump of paste, and with the right hand keep working it up the back of the hand, till all be of the proper shape and thickness.

Fortunately, Mrs Rundell takes pity on those who are not so skilful and suggests that they may either cut out top and bottom pieces and a long piece for the sides, to be fixed on to the base with egg yolk, or use a tin shape into which the pastry is fitted.

This paste can be used for pork or veal-and-ham pies, or for making a 'Goose Giblet Pie'. As recently as a generation ago this was often served at Christmas in Yorkshire. Here is Mrs Rundell's version.

> After very nicely cleaning two sets of goose giblets, stew them with a small quantity of water or well-seasoned gravy, onion, black pepper, a bunch of sweet herbs, till nearly done. Let them grow cold; and if not enough to fill the dish, lay a steak of beef or veal, or two or three mutton steaks, at the bottom.

In more traditional recipes a pudding made of goose blood is used to fill up the space in the pie. The modern 'black pudding' can easily be used instead, as follows.

> For one set of giblets use one pound of black pudding. Mix with it one small finely chopped onion, some chopped thyme and sage, a tablespoonful of shredded suet, a cupful of soft breadcrumbs, a beaten egg, salt and pepper to taste. Make forcemeat balls with the mixture and bake with the giblets and a little stock in a pie dish, covered with puff or shortcrust pastry.

Instructions for 'Gibblet Pye', complete with 'blood pudding', appear as early as 1777 in Mrs MacIver's book *Cookery and Pastry*. So while our recent version may not be elaborate enough to be classed as 'a great pye', it is a direct descendant of a very old dish.

This charming pair of cards is of a type which became very popular
as the vogue for sending Christmas cards developed in the 1860s.
An article in a contemporary Cassell's Family Magazine, describing the
work of a card factory, gives a clear picture of the rows of women workers,
each applying paper lace, scraps and little mottoes to her pile of
'cards with so many pretty borders, but blank in the centre... Some quaint cards,
evidently intended as a novelty for the children, consist of figures
which are at first represented by faces, hands and legs, but
which a nimble-fingered damsel dresses up with little stamped
velvet suits of clothes.' On the cards above the costumes are
completed with tiny metal 'buttons' and a fur muff for the lady.

WINES AND LIQUEURS

At one time no self-respecting cook or housekeeper would have lacked skill in wine-making and no festivity was complete without 'a little drop of something'—usually home-made wine or perhaps a special liqueur made to a family recipe. Sometimes the quantities proposed in old-fashioned recipes can be daunting—two hundredweight of raisins might be needed for raisin wine, or twenty quarts of French brandy, sixty oranges and two dozen lemons for Norfolk punch. But there are more modest requirements for an old favourite, cowslip wine, according to *The Englishwoman's Domestic Magazine* of April 1860.

> To two gallons of water put five pounds of powdered sugar. Boil it half an hour, and take off the scum as it rises, then pour it into a tub to cool, with the rinds of two lemons. When it is cold, add four quarts of cowslip pips to the liquor, with the juice of two lemons. Let it stand in the tub two days, stirring it every two or three hours, then put it in the barrel and let it stand for three weeks or a month, then bottle it, and put a lump of sugar in every bottle.

In the Christmas number of the same magazine (which every month aimed to provide its readers with 'a goodly variety of useful and interesting matter') we find instructions for a popular Victorian liqueur, orange shrub.

> To every five bottles of rum put the juice of thirty Seville oranges, eight or ten lemons, the peel of eight of the oranges and four lemons cut very thin, and three pounds of loaf sugar. Stir this well twice or three times a day for three or four days, then strain it through a jelly-bag and bottle it, and it will be fit for use.

Another way of making either lemon or orange shrub is to add a pound of sugar (caster is preferable) to each half-pint of strained juice. When the sugar is completely dissolved add the grated rind and a pint of rum to each half-pint of the syrup. Mix thoroughly and allow to stand for several days before bottling for use.

A good drink for winter is ginger wine which, according to Eliza Acton, is 'a very superior wine' when made with fresh cider instead of water.

> Boil together for half an hour fourteen quarts of water, twelve pounds of sugar, a quarter of a pound of best ginger bruised, and the thin rinds of six lemons. Put the whole, when milk-warm, into a clean dry cask, with the juice of the lemons and half a pound of raisins; add one large spoonful of thick yeast, and stir the wine every day for ten days. When it has ceased to ferment, add an ounce of isinglass, and a pint of brandy; bung the wine close, and in two months it will be fit to bottle, but must remain longer in the cask should it be too sweet.

An interesting recipe for ginger brandy comes from a manuscript cookery book of the 1890s; this liqueur, like shrub, can be made just a few days before it is to

Good Luck

Though other modern inventions – the telephone, steam-powered ships and locomotives, and later, of course, the motor car – appeared frequently on Christmas cards, bicycles of all kinds seem to have had the widest appeal. They gave scope not only for comic and 'surprise' designs, like the two shown here, but also for the depiction of various kinds of cycling costume. The card on the left lifts up to show a conventional greeting and the sender's name, while the card on the right folds down to reveal the unlucky cyclist's accident in the snow. Both cards are printed on heavy deckle-edged card with an embossed border, and the colour printing has remained remarkably fresh.

be drunk and could be a useful last-minute Christmas drink.

> Take not quite half an ounce of white root ginger, twelve ounces of crushed best loaf sugar or sugar candy, and the peel of one lemon to each quart of brandy. Crush the ginger thoroughly, then lay it in a jar with the sugar and thinly peeled lemon rind. Add the brandy, and let it all steep together for about a week, according to the strength of the ginger flavour required. Stir occasionally then strain and bottle.

The same writer gives instructions for making cassis, a delicious blackcurrant brandy drink, seldom found in English cookery books.

> Half fill a stone jar with ripe blackcurrants. Fill up with good brandy and cork closely. Steep thus for three weeks. Strain. Make a syrup of one pound of sugar and half a pint of boiling water. Add one pint of syrup boiling hot to each pint of currant brandy. It should be cold before bottling. Cork closely and keep for several months before using.

Perhaps one of the most popular of all home-made drinks is elderberry wine. Along with elderflower champagne, it appears in many cookery books, both old and new. But whereas it is now usually regarded as a simple country wine, it used to be, according to the Scottish writer Meg Dods, a 'rich and expensive preparation, made in the proportions of three pounds of sugar and three pints of elderberry juice to the gallon of water, enriched with chopped raisins, and perfumed and flavoured with ginger, nutmeg, cloves, &c. . . This wine is the pride of many English housewives, and no expense nor pains are spared in its preparation.' Here is a typical traditional recipe from a family cookery book.

> To four quarts of fruit (without stalks) add six quarts of boiling water. Stand for twelve to fifteen hours, then add four pounds of lump sugar. Strain three times, then boil for an hour with half a pound of large stoned Valencia raisins, a dozen or more cloves and an ounce of powdered ginger. When again cold, add a large slice of toast spread with brewer's yeast. Allow to ferment for twenty-four hours, remove the toast, strain, and skim frequently for at least four days. Bottle, adding a wine-glass of brandy to each bottle, and straining carefully as the sediment constantly re-forms.

Elderberry wine is splendid mulled—an ideal drink to offer to visitors on a cold night during the Christmas season.

WITH BEST WISHES

WITH BEST WISHES

CHRISTMAS EVE WIGS

'Wigs' are small spiced buns which originated in the west of England, but their popularity appears to have spread for they sometimes appear in early recipe books from other parts of the country. Like the more familiar hot cross buns, they were made from a yeast dough, enriched with eggs and spices. Their curious name refers to the 'wedge' or triangular shape in which they were once made. Like the special Christmas 'kitchel' or cake of eastern England, and the Coventry 'God-cakes', they symbolized the Trinity and were once associated with religious festivals. In some eighteenth-century recipes wigs are made from 'meal well dryed by ye fire', but in the following, 'To make good Wigs', taken from a manuscript cookery book of 1718, white or 'fine' flour is used.

Take a quarter of a peck of fine flour rub into it three quarters of a pound of fresh Butter till 'tis like grated bread, something more than half a pound of sugar, half a nutmeg, and half a race of genger grated, three Eggs yolks & white beaten very well & put to them half a pint of thick Ale yeast & three or four spoonfuls of sack, make a hole in your flour and pour in your yeast and eggs and as much milk just warm as will make it into a light paste let it stand before the fire to rise half an hour then make it into a Dozen & half of wigs, wash them all over with egg just as they go into the oven, a quick oven and half an hour will bake them.

The inclusion of sack, a sweet Spanish wine, must have given a rich flavour and heavy texture. Later in the century Hannah Glasse uses sack, with thick cream instead of milk and caraway comfits in place of ginger—an even richer mixture. She also gives a simplified version leaving out all the spices, these 'Light Wigs' being much more like the scones that we eat today.

Take a pound and a half of flour, and half a pint of milk made warm, mix these together, cover it up, and let it lye by the fire half an hour; then take half a pound of sugar and half a pound of butter, then work these into a paste and make it into wigs, with as little flour as possible. Let the

Here two small scrap cards feature Santa Claus at his most pagan-looking, bearing a bunch of spruce and crowned with berried holly. The bright colours of the scraps are set against paper-lace backgrounds, typical of the 1870s. The red-edged visiting-card, with its seasonal decoration and greeting, is well preserved; while the design of roses and cherubs is still in its original paper frame, which would probably have been attached at one side of a larger card to form a hinge.

oven be pretty quick, and they will rise very much. Mind to mix a quarter of a pint of good ale yeast in the milk.

For festive occasions, however, spices were always included. Meanwhile the shape of wigs changed from triangular to round, and they were often baked in greased saucers or patty-pans instead of on the 'well-flowered' paper of earlier days. Like many other traditional foods, wigs are not to be found in the popular cookery books of the Victorian era. Continental influences and a growing preoccupation with diet and nutrition meant that many such old recipes were more likely to be written in family recipe books or passed on by word of mouth. Even though the sweet wine has disappeared, the method and ingredients for wigs in the following recipe, handed down over four generations, differ surprisingly little from those of the early eighteenth century.

Take five eggs, two ounces of yeast, two pounds of flour, half a pound of butter, half a pound of sugar, a pinch of salt, one ounce of caraway seeds, one teaspoonful of grated nutmeg, three or four tablespoonsful of cream or slightly warmed milk. Cream the yeast with a little of the milk, sprinkle with flour and stand to 'sponge' in a warm place for about fifteen minutes. Rub the butter into the flour and salt, then add the sugar, nutmeg and caraway. Add the beaten eggs together with the yeast mixture to the flour, with enough milk or cream to make a soft dough. Mix well, then set to rise till doubled in size. Shape into buns, prove, and bake for about twenty minutes in a fairly hot oven.

Wigs are still made in the West Country using a conventional scone mixture and no yeast, with caraway seeds and candied peel added. These are served on Christmas Eve along with ale or mulled elderberry wine or with cider 'hotted up'. It is not so very long ago that farmers in Devon and Somerset faithfully observed the ancient ritual of 'wassailing' their apple trees on Christmas Eve. A hot cake and some cider would usually be offered to the chief apple-tree in the orchard to ensure a good crop of fruit in the year to come.

These Christmas verses woven on silk are possibly the work of Thomas Stevens of Coventry. Framed with borders of silver paper lace, they were intended to be mounted on a folded paper 'card', perhaps with an embossed or cut-out surround in the same oval shape. The wording is typically sentimental, with an emphasis upon the old-fashioned customs of the season as well as upon its religious significance.

SHORTBREAD

Shortbread is a familiar delicacy both at Christmas and Hogmanay, when it is served with drinks to guests or sent as a welcome gift.

It is thought to have a long history dating back to the days when special 'bannocks'—round flat cakes of oatmeal—were baked for festive occasions of all kinds in Scotland. The Yule bannock for Christmas morning would have a dual significance, celebrating the birth of the Christ child and also the midwinter festival. It was gradually replaced by the more familiar and much richer shortbread, recipes for which appear in most nineteenth-century cookery books, both Scottish and English. Here is Mrs Dalgairns's recipe for a rich shortbread.

> For two pounds of sifted flour allow one pound of butter, salt or fresh; a quarter of a pound of candied orange and lemon peel; of pounded loaf sugar, blanched sweet almonds, and caraway comfits, a quarter of a pound each; cut the lemon, the orange-peel, and almonds into small thin bits, and mix them with a pound and a half of the flour, a few of the caraway comfits, and the sugar; melt the butter, and when cool, pour it clear from the sediment into the flour, at the same time mixing it quickly. With the hands, form it into a large round of nearly an inch thick, using the remainder of the flour to make it up with; cut it into four, and with the finger and thumb pinch each bit neatly round the edge; prick them with a fork, and strew the rest of the caraway comfits over the top. Put the pieces upon the white paper dusted with flour, and then upon tins. Bake them in a moderate oven.

The caraway comfits used here were sugared caraway seeds, which may be replaced by plain ones, and caster sugar may be used instead of loaf sugar. For plain shortbread Mrs Dalgairns suggests the same proportions of flour and butter with a little sugar, but omits the sweetmeats and almonds. It should be mixed as above but rolled out a little thinner than the rich shortbread and pricked with a fork. Fifty years later than Mrs Dalgairns the English cook Eliza Acton gives her version of 'Good Scottish Shortbread'. She comments that 'This to many persons is a very indigestible compound, though agreeable to the taste'.

> With one pound of flour mix well two ounces of sifted sugar and one of candied orange-rind or citron sliced small; make these into a paste with from eight to nine ounces of good butter, made sufficiently warm to be liquid; press the paste together with the hands and mould it upon tins into large cakes nearly an inch thick, pinch the edges, and bake in a moderate oven for twenty minutes, or longer should it not be quite crisp, but do not allow it to become deeply coloured.

A different kind of rich shortbread is still made in Ayrshire using cream and egg and omitting the candied peels and caraway. This recipe can be used for making the traditional 'petticoat tails', thought to be so called either on account of their shape—like that of the once fashionable petticoats of court ladies—or being a corruption of the French *petits galettes*—little cakes.

> Four ounces each of flour, rice flour and butter, two ounces of caster sugar, one of egg and one tablespoon of cream.
> Mix together the flour and rice flour, then rub in the butter. Add the sugar, make a well into which put the egg and cream. Form a paste and knead on a sugared board until smooth. Roll to a thickness of half an inch, and cut into rounds with a cutter; for petticoat tails cut into a large round, using a plate, then cut a smaller round in the centre; divide the larger circle into eight, and bake with the smaller one on greased paper on a baking-sheet, in a hot oven for 10–15 minutes, or until golden brown. Sprinkle sugar over the tops when taking the biscuits from the oven; cool a little before lifting them from the baking-sheet.

It is interesting to find that Eliza Acton's recipe for a 'galette'—'a favourite cake in France'—is similar to the Ayrshire shortbread given above.

> Work lightly three-quarters of a pound of butter into a pound of flour, add a large saltspoonful of salt, and make these into a paste with the yolks of a couple of eggs mixed with a small cupful of good cream; roll this into a complete round, three-quarters of an inch thick; score it in small diamonds, brush yolk of egg over the top, and bake for about half an hour in a tolerably quick oven; it is usually eaten hot but is served cold also. An ounce of sifted sugar is sometimes added to it.

She adds that this is a 'good galette', whereas a 'common' one takes only six or eight ounces of butter to a pound of flour, and water is used to mix instead of eggs and cream. All cooks seem to agree however that for a good shortbread, however plain, the best quality butter should be used.

...prom... ...Son,
...him all glor... ...living
On this fa... ...Christmas morn.
Oh, ma... ...is peace upon you rest,
And al... ...your future life invest !

This elaborate white and gold card was probably produced in the 1890s.
Mounted on a card base which provides a gilded frame, the doors open
to reveal embossed figures of angels surrounding the infant Christ.
The angels' wings sparkle with frosting and when the silk ribbon is pulled,
enabling the figures to move down, a star and cherubs appear above
the group. With its appropriate verse this card forms
a charming reminder of the religious significance of
Chtistmas morning.

CANDIES AND BONBONS

Traditionally every child's Christmas stocking contains some sweets or candy, but sugar and chocolate have only become widely available since the seventeenth century, and it was really the Victorians who developed the skills of making the kinds of sweet we still know today. Barley-sugar, toffee and nougat were early favourites, but for very special occasions crystallized fruits were made at home. These were already popular in the eighteenth century when recipes for candied flowers and fruit appeared in most books of cookery or housekeeping. Here is Mrs MacIver's charming recipe of 1777, 'To Candy Flowers'.

Take any kind of flowers you think pretty; if the stalks are very long, cut off some of them; clarify and boil a pound of fine sugar till near candy height; when the sugar begins to grow stiff, and something cool, dip the flowers into it; take them out immediately, and lay them one by one on a sieve; dry them in a stove.

Later, in an Edwardian booklet *Prize Recipes*, pears and oranges, apricots, greengages and plums are recommended as suitable fruits to crystallize. 'These are much used at Christmas and are much cheaper if done at home,' states the author with an admirable sense of economy.

The fruits must be firm and not too ripe. Remove the skins, and cut any fruit containing stones in half and remove the stones, pare and remove stalks from small pears. Roll the fruit in castor sugar that contains a small saltspoonful each of cream of tartar and bicarbonate of soda to every pound. Pack separately on a dish and cover with sugar. Bake in a hot oven until fruit is tender; remove the dish, stand it in a cool larder, and before the fruit is set cold roll in the sugar mixture again and stand on a wire rack for twenty-four hours, then place in a box or tin with greaseproof paper between the layers.

As well as sugar-plums wrapped in silver paper, a lucky child might receive the familiar twisted sticks of barley sugar. To judge by the number of recipes that appear in cookery books from the eighteenth century onwards this was one of the most popular candies, as well as one of the simplest to make.

Take twelve ounces of loaf sugar, a quarter of a pint of water, and half the white of one egg. Boil all together. When it commences to candy, add one teaspoonful of lemon juice. Boil it quickly till it again begins to candy, butter a dish and pour the mixture thinly over it. As it cools cut it into thin strips, and twist it in the form of sticks.

Barley sugar was often used to make bonbons, either in the form of simple sugar drops flavoured with lemon or cinnamon or the more elaborate 'Palace Bonbons', as in the following recipe from Eliza Acton.

Take some fine fresh candied orange-rind, or citron, clear off the sugar which adheres to it, cut it into inch-squares, stick these singly on the prong of a silver fork or on osier-twigs, dip them into liquid barley-sugar, and place them on a dish rubbed with the smallest possible quantity of very pure salad oil. When cold, put them into tin boxes or canisters well dried, with paper, which should also be very dry, between each layer.

To make a simple form of nougat, liquid barley sugar was mixed with dried blanched almonds and set in a

A favourite novelty of the 1860s was the sachet card. Usually this contained a scented pad within a false envelope which unfolded to show a picture or message. Reminiscent of the popular perfumed valentines with their gilding and embossed borders, the Christmas sachet was often distinguished from them by a suitable scrap, like this one of children playing round a present-laden tree. Though decorated trees did not become part of the Christmas scene until made popular by Prince Albert, it was not long before they appeared frequently on greetings cards.

greased mould, while another favourite delicacy was made by dipping almonds or other nuts into melted chocolate mixed with an equal quantity of powdered sugar. Chocolate drops were formed from the same mixture, but a more elaborate and antiquated way of making chocolate bonbons appeared in Dolby's *Cook's Dictionary*.

> Put a quarter of a pound of chocolate over a fire, to dissolve it; having boiled two pounds of sugar till it 'pearls', put a spoonful or two into the chocolate; stir till it forms a thin paste and then pour it on the sugar and boil both together to a caramel. In the meantime melt a little butter, skim and pour it off clear into a basin; take a spoonful of it and rub it with your hand over a marble slab or table: on this pour the chocolate and sugar; then take two ends of a sword-blade (one in each hand) and press lines an inch apart all down it; cross them in like manner so as to mark the sugar in small squares all over; doing it as quickly as possible, lest the sugar should cool before you have done; then pass the sword-blade between the marble and the sugar; lay under the latter sheets of paper; and when cold, break it into pieces according to the marks, and wrap each square in paper.

The modern palette knife seems a poor substitute for a sword-blade, but the most important factor in this kind of sweet-making is speed so, provided that the markings are evenly made before the mixture sets too hard, it should be possible to manage with any kind of reasonably long knife. Plain dark chocolate is preferable and a heavy pan should be used for making this and other candies. Commercially-made sweets may perhaps look more glamorous, but old-fashioned home-made confectionery can be an unusual and delicious gift for grown-ups as well as children, especially at Christmas.

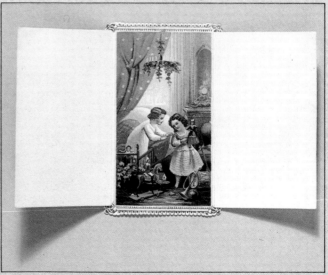

This three-fold card is a typical product of the 1870s. Mounted on an embossed and gilt-edged visiting card, it appears at first to be a conventional floral card. The doors open, however, to reveal first a Christmas Eve scene then one for Christmas morning. The sentimental pictures, first of sleeping children surrounded by angels and later showing each other their toys, are truly Victorian in spirit.

GINGERBREADS

For many centuries gingerbread has been associated with festivals and gift-giving. Although we no longer gild it with gold leaf, as did cooks in Elizabethan times, it is often iced and decorated with candied peel or made into fairings for special occasions. Gingerbread baked in wooden moulds was often given as presents and children still love to find gingerbread 'men' in their Christmas stockings or at parties. In early recipes honey was used and the mixture was always heavily spiced. Here are Thomas Shoesmith's directions for 'Queen's Gingerbread', taken from his *Biscuit-baker's and Pastrycook's Assistant*.

> Take two pounds of honey, one pound and threequarters of the best moist sugar, three pounds of flour, half a pound of sweet almonds blanched and cut thin, half a pound of candied orange peel, the rind of two lemons grated, one ounce of powdered cinnamon, half an ounce each of nutmeg, cloves, mace and cardamons, mixed and powdered and a wineglassful of water: put your honey, sugar and water into a pan over a fire, and make it quite hot; mix the other ingredients into the flour and pour in your honey, sugar and water, and mix it all well together; let it stand till next day: make it into cakes and bake it.

These ingredients could be halved and treacle or golden syrup substituted for honey. Usually a steady heat is recommended for baking gingerbreads but a hotter oven is better for baking the small 'Ginger Cakes' of the following recipe. This comes from *The Healthful Cookery Book* of 1812; the cakes are in fact rather like the present-day biscuits, and again the quantities could be halved.

> With four pounds of flour mix four ounces of ginger powdered very fine, heap them in a dish and make a hole in the middle; then beat six eggs and put them into a saucepan with a pint of cream, two pounds of butter, and a pound of powdered sugar. Stir them together over a slow fire till the butter is entirely melted, and then pour it to the flour and ginger. Make it up into a paste, and roll it out till it is about a quarter of an inch thick, then cut it into cakes with the top of a cup or glass. They must be baked in a very hot oven.

Just before the Great War, economy was the keynote of Edwardian pamphlets of popular cookery. One writer includes a recipe for ginger biscuits with the comment that 'these are easily made, very economical and always please the young people'.

> One pound of flour, four ounces of lard or butter, one teaspoon carbonate of soda, two teaspoon ground ginger, a pinch of salt. Well mix in the dry state, then bind together with a teaspoon of milk and four of golden syrup.

This mixture may be used to make either round biscuits or gingerbread men, which should be baked quickly and left on the baking sheet until cold.

Ginger nuts have remained popular but like other forms of gingerbread have tended to become less elaborate in recent times. The Victorians, however, still made them in traditional fashion, well spiced and enriched with candied fruit. The following recipe for 'Rich Sweetmeat Gingerbread Nuts' comes from *The Englishwoman's Domestic Magazine* of 1850.

> Put a pound of good treacle into a basin, and pour over it a quarter of a pound of clarified butter, or fresh butter, melted so as not to oil, and one pound of coarse brown sugar. Stir the whole well. While mixing, add an ounce each of candied orange peel and candied angelica, and a quarter of an ounce of candied lemon peel, cut into very minute pieces, but not bruised or pounded, with half an ounce of pounded coriander seeds, and half an ounce of caraway seeds. Having mixed them thoroughly together, break in an egg, and work the whole up with as much flour as may be necessary to form a fine paste, which is to be made into nuts of any size. Put on the bare tin plate and set in a rather brisk oven.

In earlier times, such rich gingerbread would have been stamped with a pattern after being rolled out—yet another way of making it an acceptable gift.

And may it bring the very thing
You long for this most happy day.

These two cheerful Christmas postcards date from about 1910
and were produced by the well-known firm of Faulkner, successors to the
earlier Hildersheimer and Faulkner who produced many of the most popular
Victorian greetings cards. The artist, Agnes Richardson, was one
of a large number of contemporary women designers and her cards often
featured rosy-cheeked children in the Mabel Lucy Attwell style
which became so popular after the Great War. Conventional Christmas
decoration is almost entirely absent from these two examples,
which rely upon the verbal message and the theme of presents
and stockings to convey a seasonal atmosphere.

THE BOAR'S HEAD

The bore's head in hande bring I,
With garlands gay and rosemary.

The words of the original Boar's Head Carol, printed in 1521 but already part of a long tradition, go on to say that this great dish was always served with mustard, for it was in fact what is better known as brawn—pig's head soused in pickle and garnished with herbs. The head of the wild boar would have been an impressive sight and feasting upon it the reward for the dangers of hunting. It was brought in on a gold or silver dish to a fanfare of trumpets and the singing of the famous carol, and this ceremony has remained till the present day as part of Christmas celebrations at New College, Oxford.

The following instructions for preparing and decorating a boar's head are taken from a collection of Old English recipes compiled in the early 1920s.

Prepare a mixture of one and a half pounds of salt, a tablespoon of saltpetre, and a little brown sugar and some aromatic spices. Remove the bones from the head, and rub it with one-sixth of the mixture each day for six days. Then remove the ears, as these must be cooked separately. Stuff the head with a forcemeat composed of very finely minced pork, and veal, truffles, champignons, four ounces of breadcrumbs, and bind together with two eggs, season with spice pepper and salt. A very large head may have a bullock's tongue in the centre with the stuffing round. Tie into shape with a cloth, putting a flat plate at the back of the head, and boil gently in stock for five or six hours. Take up and press the head into shape, and let it get quite cold. Cook the ears for an hour only and put them in place when cold, and make sockets for the glass eyes. Give two or three coats of glaze, put in the eyes and decorate with some butter through a forcer.

By mid-Victorian times, when Alexis Soyer was producing elaborate menus for the Reform Club in London, the wild boar had long been extinct in Britain. The great chef, however, devised a dish of 'Pig's Head in Imitation of Wild Boar's Head'; this 'was much approved of both for its ferocious appearance, and its flavour, and it lasted good for three weeks'. After lying in pickle for ten days the head was stuffed with six to eight pounds of pork forcemeat as well as fillets of meat from the neck, so must have been very large indeed. Then it was braised for eight hours before being glazed and decorated with currants for eyes, tusks made of pastry, and some 'very fresh tulips and roses stuck tastefully in the ears'. This must have been a summer dish; instead of

flowers the Christmas boar's head would have been garlanded with rosemary, bay and holly, with an apple or orange placed in its open jaws. Here is Soyer's recipe for 'Boar's Head Sauce'.

Cut the rind (free from pith) of two Seville oranges into very thin strips half an inch in length, which blanch in boiling water, drain them upon a sieve, and put them in a basin, with a spoonful of mixed English mustard, four of currant jelly, a little pepper, salt (mix well together), and half a pint of good port wine.

In Ireland the traditional dish of pig's face used always to appear, like the English boar's head and the Scottish haggis, at times of feasting and celebration. It was cooked fresh and served hot, usually with cabbage; after boiling the rind was made crisp and golden at the fire. The following more sophisticated version appears in *The Cook and Housewife's Manual* by Meg Dods.

Make the head as large as you can, by cutting down to the shoulders. Singe it carefully. Put a red-hot poker into the ears. Clean and carefully bone the head without breaking the skin. Rub it with salt, and pour a boiled cold brine over it, with a large handful of juniper berries, a few bruised cloves and four bay-leaves, with thyme, basil, sage, a head of garlic bruised, and a half-ounce of saltpetre pounded. Let the head steep in this for ten days, and turn it and rub it often. Then wipe, drain and dry it, and make a forcemeat for it thus:— Take equal quantities of undressed ham and the breast of bacon. Season highly with cook's-pepper and fine spices if you choose. Pound the meat very small, and mix it with some seasoned lard, parsley and young onions finely mixed.

The stuffed head is sewn up and tied in a cloth, then stewed with vegetables and served cold. Not quite so splendid as the original boar's head perhaps but nevertheless 'Pig's Face Stuffed' is, claims the author, 'a dish well worth the attention of the gourmand and of the country housekeeper'.

Although wild boar became extinct in Britain during the seventeenth century, brawn has continued to be made up to the present time. The meat from a pig's head and feet is spiced and pickled, then flattened and rolled up tightly; it is then boiled with herbs and vegetables and served cold. A favourite dish in Victorian times, it often appeared alongside the decorated ham at the Christmas table.

Many cards of the 1870s and 1880s reflected the Victorian delight
in any aspect of the old-fashioned Christmas. Just as seasonal
verses often mentioned the feasting and dancing of earlier times,
so numerous cards like these showed different costumes and
activities in what was thought to be a mediaeval style.

This is a production of the firm of Marcus Ward which greatly expanded
the English card trade, commissioning many well-known artists
including Walter Crane and Kate Greenaway. The picture here is
of a Christmas reconciliation and it bears a moral message above.

An unusual card shows a monk on a donkey; he seems to be turning
his back on the knight's and ladies' merry-making. The humorous
effect here is strangely modern.

These cards are printed on gold backgrounds in colours which are
still very bright and fresh. Though small, they are both
effective and interesting designs.

ROAST GOOSE FOR CHRISTMAS DAY

Roasted birds of all kinds were eaten at the earliest Christmas feasts. The most spectacular of these was the peacock, which was skinned and cooked, then dressed up again in its own feathers and served with its beak and feet heavily gilded and colourful tail spread wide. The flesh, however, was later considered coarse and tasteless, unlike that of the 'savoury goose' which continued to be a favourite dish, especially in Scotland. Its preparation has changed little over the centuries: sage and onion stuffing to hide the often rank flavour of a bird which might be hung up to a fortnight before cooking, and apple sauce to counteract the large amount of fat have remained the standard re-commendation of cookery books. In the eighteenth century Mrs Hannah Glasse issued the caution to 'never put onion into anything unless you are sure every body loves it; take care that your goose be clean picked and washed', but she was something of an exception. Her contemporary Mrs MacIver states that 'a goose or duck is the better of being rubbed with pepper and salt within'. This was a standard way of disguising the 'high' flavour of meat, and Mrs MacIver also suggests salting the outside of the goose two or three days before it is roasted. Then 'dish up the goose with gravy-sauce, and garnish it with raw onions; send up a plateful of applesauce along with it'.

Later, in the nineteenth century, Meg Dods claims that the use of raw onions is old-fashioned and gives the following instructions for preparing and stuffing a goose for Christmas.

After the goose is carefully picked and singed, let it be well washed and dried with a cloth. Stuffing—Four well-sized onions, about half their weight in sage undried, and half the liver; parboil slightly, and chop these very fine: Add a bit of butter, yolk of an egg, the crumbs of a penny loaf or an equal quantity of mashed potatoes, and season rather highly with pepper and salt. With this stuff the goose. Spit the goose; fasten tightly at neck and rump. Paper the breast, but remove the paper when it has swelled. A goose requires a brisk fire, well kept up; and will take from two hours to two and a half to roast. The breast must not be allowed to sink.

A more sophisticated method of stuffing and spit-roasting a goose is described in detail in Soyer's *Modern Housewife*—a classic mid-Victorian cookery book.

Peel and cut in rather small dice six middle-sized onions, put in a pan, with two ounces of butter, half a teaspoonful of salt, a quarter ditto of pepper, a little grated nutmeg and sugar, six leaves of fresh sage chopped fine, put on fire, stir with wooden spoon till pulp, then have the goose ready trussed, and stuff it whilst hot, tie the skin of the neck to the back, pass the spit through, and roast two hours before a moderate fire. . . I have tried it with the liver chopped and mixed it with the onions; I also at times add two cold potatoes cut in dice and a spoonful of rice added to the former stuffing, and occasionally breadcrumbs; it removes the richness of the fat, and renders it more palatable and digestive; and I also sometimes add twenty chestnuts cut into dice.

In spite of the influence upon English cooking of famous French chefs like Soyer, the continental practice of fattening geese to produce more liver did not become established in England. The goose remained a farmhouse product destined chiefly for roasting or pies; whilst the liver was considered too strong for English palates, the giblets were used for soup or pies and the blood was often mixed with oatmeal to make 'blood pudding', a favourite Yorkshire dish until recent times. Always the emphasis was upon seasoning, as in this 'Savoury Sauce for a roasted Goose' of 1807.

A table spoonful of made mustard, half a teaspoonful of Cayenne pepper, and three spoonfuls of port wine. When mixed, pour this (hot) into the body of the goose, by a slit in the apron, just before sending it up. . . This is a 'Secret worth knowing'. It wonderfully improves the sage and onion.

Named after its original author, this 'Dr Hunter's Sauce' was destined to appear again and again in nineteenth-century recipe books. Only ten years after its first appearance Dr Kichener, the author of *The Cook's Oracle*, adds the comment 'or, as all the company may not like it, stir it into a quarter of a pint of thick melted butter, or thickened Gravy, and send it up in a Boat'. He also gives a recipe for 'Sauce Robert' which was to remain popular throughout Victorian times and was often served with roast goose or pork.

> Put an ounce of Butter into a pint Stewpan; when it is melted, add to it half an ounce of Onion minced very fine: turn it with a wooden spoon, till it takes a light brown colour, then stir in a tablespoonful of Mushroom Catsup (with or without the like quantity of Port wine), half a pint of Broth, or water, and a quarter of a teaspoonful of Pepper, the same of Salt, give them a boil, then add a teaspoonful of Mustard, and the juice of half a Lemon, or one or two teaspoonfuls of Vinegar, or Basil, Tarragon or Burnet Vinegar.

The 'mushroom catsup' which appears in this and so many other old-fashioned recipes was a concentrated essence of mushrooms. A spoonful of finely chopped or pounded fresh mushrooms could be used instead. The addition of vinegar or lemon juice helped to offset the richness of the goose in the same way as did the more familiar apple sauce, which, in spite of Victorian preferences, was to outlast its rivals and remains the accepted accompaniment to the Christmas goose.

In spite of the fashion for a Christmas dinner of roast turkey, geese seem to appear far more often upon greetings cards. They are usually associated with snow, perhaps because of the charming old story that flakes of snow were really goose feathers floating down from the sky. On this postcard, dated 1909, the goose-girl is clearly a fairy-tale character. The card is of a much less sentimental design than is usual for the period: its red, black and white colouring upon a grey ground makes it more attractive and interesting than many conventional cards.

ALDERMAN IN CHAINS

The picturesque description of a plump well-roasted turkey as a city alderman surrounded by a chain of office composed of savoury pork sausages has never been bettered. Well fattened, comfortably seated on the largest platter, and borne in with much ceremony to the family dinner-table, the turkey came into its own in Victorian times when the fashion for lavish Christmas festivities was enthusiastically revived. But turkeys and capons had in fact been part of the menu for great feasts since the time of Henry VIII. *The Healthful Cookery Book* of 1812 gives the following directions 'To roast a Turkey Capon or Fowl as practised in the royal Kitchen in the Reign of Queen Anne'.

> When the turkey, capon or fowl has been long enough at the fire to be thoroughly hot, so as to require basting, baste it once all over very well with fresh butter, then in a minute after dredge it thinly all over with flour. The heat of the fire will convert this into a thin crust which will keep the juice of the meat, therefore it is not to be basted any more; nor any thing done till it is almost roasted sufficiently. Then baste it well with butter as before, on which the crust will give way and fall off. As the meat begins to brown, sprinkle it with a little large salt, and let it do till the outside is a nice brown. It was sometimes the custom to baste such meats with the yolks of fresh laid eggs, beaten thin, which was to be continued all the time of roasting.

Although this last suggestion sounds rather laborious it must have given better protection to the tender flesh of the bird, which was particularly at risk when spit-roasted. The art of roasting meat over the fire was anything but simple if we are to believe Dr Kichener, who devotes a whole chapter to it in his *Cook's Oracle,* saying that 'A Good Cook is as anxiously attentive to the appearance and Colour of her Roasts, as a Court Beauty is to her Complexion at a Birthday Ball'. He also warns housewives that 'many a Christmas dinner has been spoiled by the Turkey having been hung up in a cold larder, becoming thoroughly frozen—Jack Frost has ruined the reputation of many a TurkeyRoaster'. To avoid a tough bird it should not be dressed, so he claims, till at least four or five days (in cold weather, eight or ten) after it has been killed. Here is Dr Kichener's recipe for turkey stuffing; nearly two centuries later, it is still perfectly usable.

> Mince a quarter of a pound of Beef Suet (Beef Marrow is better), the same weight of Bread Crumbs, two drachms of Parsley leaves, a drachm and a half of sweet Marjoram (or Lemon-thyme), and the same of grated Lemon peel, and Onion or Eshallot, chopped as fine as possible, a little grated Nutmeg, Pepper and Salt: pound thoroughly together with the yolk and white of two Eggs.

A drachm was about equivalent to a medium-sized teaspoonful and the above quantities would be sufficient for a small turkey; for a large one the stuffing is mixed with an equal quantity of pork sausage-meat. The Doctor adds that 'Fried pork sausages are a very savoury and favourite accompaniment to either roasted or boiled Poultry. A Turkey, thus garnished, is called an "Alderman in Chains".'

Later in the century Alexis Soyer, giving his version of 'Plain Roasted Turkey with Sausages', comments rather pompously that 'This well-known dish, which has the joyous recollection of Christmas attached to it, and its well-known cognomen of "an alderman in chains", brings to our minds eye the famed hospitality of this mighty city'. As *chef de cuisine* of the Reform Club he indulged in sophisticated sauces made with truffles, mushrooms or oysters, rejecting with distaste the more common bread sauce. However he does give a simpler chestnut stuffing for turkey.

> I put two pounds of sausage meat in a basin with a little grated nutmeg; I then take two tablespoonfuls of chopped onions, put them in a saute-pan with a little butter, and let them do for two minutes, which add to the meat, also two eggs well beaten up and a quarter of a pint of white sauce if at hand, and fifteen fine roasted chestnuts; add this to the stuffing, and fill the bird as usual, not too full at the breast.

To the gravy, he suggests adding a glass of sherry as well as 'fifty button onions previously stewed, and twentyfive roasted chestnuts'. Other cooks preferred to cut up the chestnuts for the sauce, adding a glass of white wine.

White wine was also used with oysters, which for a long time seem to have been more popular than chestnuts for sauces and stuffings. The following recipe for 'A Turkey with Oysters' comes from the eighteenth-century *Powell's Family Companion*.

> Take half a pint of Water, half an Anchovy, three Spoonfuls of Oyster-Liquor, thicken it well with Flower over the Fire, then Stew your Oysters with the rest of the liquor, and two blades of Mace, a little whole Pepper, then take out your Oysters, and strain all the Liquor. When your Turkey is almost ready, put all your sauce together, with a piece of Butter, and a spoonful or two of gravy, a spoonful of white Wine, a little Lemon Juice, and shake it over the Fire, and Pour it over the Turkey, and serve it up.

'Cat' cards of all kinds were much in demand towards the end of the century.
They were appreciated by adults as well as by children, often depicting cats
involved in human activities like the feline cook roasting chestnuts (top).
This is delicately coloured on heavy gilt-edged card, but the folding card (above)
is altogether more sophisticated in feeling. This is one of many designs
by Louis Wain produced for Raphael Tuck and Sons in the 1890s.
His rather acid sense of humour did not appeal to everyone, especially as he
often showed cats merrily carousing and rather the worse for wear,
but his designs provide a welcome antidote
to Victorian sentimentality.

PLUMB PORRIDGE

Plumb porridge, the original Christmas pudding, is yet another dish thought to go back to ancient times, when the winter festival was celebrated by the consumption of large quantities of gruel or 'brose'. Later, heavily spiced and often laced with alcohol, this 'pottage' was further enriched by the addition of sugar and all kinds of dried fruits; but round about 1700 it was superseded by the now familiar 'plumb pudding'. Sweet puddings, either baked or boiled in special cloths, were by this time becoming popular and were served not only with the meat course (like our present-day Yorkshire pudding) but as a course on their own. Suet or bone-marrow were often used to thicken these early puddings, whereas breadcrumbs seem to have been more popular for stiffening the meat broth which formed the foundation for plumb porridge.

A few recipes for plumb porridge still appeared in eighteenth-century cookery books, usually amongst the soups and broths. Here is Mrs MacIver's version of 'Plumb Pottage' 1773.

Take a hough of beef and a knuckle of veal, put them on the fire in a close pot, with six or seven Scots pints of water; take out the veal before it is over-boiled, and let the beef boil till the whole substance is out of it; strain off the stock, and then put in the crumbs of a two-penny loaf, two pounds of currants well clean'd, two pounds of raisins ston'd, and one pound of prunes. Let all boil together till they swell; then warm the veal, and put it in the middle of the dish.

Perhaps because of its Celtic origin, plumb porridge came to be regarded as a Scottish speciality. Meg Dods included an almost identical recipe to Mrs MacIver's in *The Cook and Housewife's Manual* in her section on Scottish National Dishes, but it is in the English recipe book of Mrs Glasse that we find 'To Make Plumb Porridge for Christmas'.

Take a leg and shin of beef, put to them eight gallons of water and boil them till they are very tender, and when the broth is strong strain it out; wipe the pot and put in the broth again; then slice six penny loaves thin, cut off the top and bottom, put some of the liquor to it, cover it up and let it stand a quarter of an hour, boil it and strain it, and then put it in your pot. Let it boil a quarter of an hour, then put in five pounds of currants clean washed and picked; let them boil a little, and put in five pounds of raisins of the sun stoned, and two pounds of Prunes, and let them boil till they swell; then put in three quarters of an ounce of mace, half an ounce of cloves, two nutmegs, all

of them beat fine, and mix it with a little liquor cold, and put them in a very little while, and take off the pot; then put in three pounds of sugar, a little salt, a quart of sack, a quart of claret, and the juice of two or three lemons. You may thicken with sago, instead of bread, if you please. You must boil two pounds of prunes in a quart of water till they are tender, and strain them into the pot, when it is boiling.

Such quantities were clearly intended for a large household, just as in the nineteenth century plum puddings were usually made several at a time in anticipation of Christmas visitors. Mrs Glasse gives more modest recipes for plumb porridge made from barley broth, currants and raisins, and for plumb gruel made from oatmeal and currants. These were intended as Lenten dishes omitting the meat and including only one glass of white wine and a scraping of nutmeg, in contrast to the pints of sack and claret and heavy seasoning of the Christmas version.

No one knows exactly why plumb porridge was overtaken in popularity by plum pudding, but it is clear that for a time the two coexisted quite happily. Both appeared on the laden tables of the Christmas feasts provided by landlords for their tenants in the eighteenth century, but in his *Popular Antiquities* the scholar William Brand noted: 'I dined at the chaplain's table at St James's on Christmas Day, 1801, and partook of the first thing served and eaten on that festival at that table, i.e. a tureen full of rich luscious plum-porridge, I do not know that the custom is any where else retained.'

Perhaps eventually cooks tired of all the straining and stirring and so went over to the pre-mixing of fruit, breadcrumbs and wine, as with other sweet puddings; or, as one theory has it, perhaps someone simply let the porridge boil dry one day and found the resulting mixture even more palatable than usual. Certainly the practice of boiling puddings in a cloth alongside the meat in a large pot goes back to the early days of puddings; and it was the boiling method rather than baking in the oven which was to become the usual one for Christmas puddings. Plumb porridge lost its favoured place beside the roasted birds and mince-pies to reappear only briefly in the Christmas verses which were part of the Victorians' nostalgia for the old-time festivities.

Another Raphael Tuck production, this Edwardian folding card contains the kind of Christmas surprise
so often featured on cards intended specially for children. Although far less elaborate than
some of the animated cards of earlier times, the pop-up type became popular and, printed on
heavy card like this one, was much less fragile for children to handle. Rats and mice often appeared
as part of Christmas designs, usually with a cat in pursuit; here they are sentimentally drawn, but
quite often dead animals and birds accompanied the seasonal greetings, with a morbid effect that seems
to have had considerable appeal a hundred years ago.

PLUM PUDDINGS

'There are a thousand other ways of making plum-pudding,' declared Meg Dods, before giving her readers of the 1820s instructions for 'A superfine Plum-Pudding'. Not only printed cookery books but also those compiled and laboriously written out by cooks from the seventeenth century on contain recipes for this mixture of suet and spices, fruit, eggs and alcohol; along with roast beef it became a national symbol as well as an integral part of the English Christmas.

At first the recipes were comparatively simple. As late as 1773, in *Cookery and Pastry*, Mrs MacIver places her version next to 'A boil'd custard pudding' and 'A plain suet pudding', neither of which sounds at all festive or exciting; but her plum pudding contains all the familiar ingredients.

> Stone and shred a pound of raisins; pick and clean a pound of currants; mince a pound of suet; beat eight eggs with four spoonfuls of flour till it is very smooth; put in a little salt; season it with cinnamon and nutmeg, and a gill of brandy; mix all well together, and tie them up very hard; put in a pot of boiling water; it will take four hours boiling.

'A very Small Very Rich Plum Pudding' comes from *The Healthful Cookery Book* of 1812. Although the author of this is full of advice about dried fruit and spices being injurious to delicate constitutions, she admits that they are too popular to be left out; and though brandy is omitted wine sauce is allowed.

> Three quarters of a pound of suet, shred small, half a pound of raisins, weigh them after they are stoned, and chop them a little, three spoonfuls of moist sugar, a little nutmeg and salt, three yolks of eggs, and two whites. Let it boil four hours in a basin or tin mould, well buttered. Pour over it, when served up, melted butter with white wine and sugar.

Though rich, this is what Mrs Dods would have termed 'A Common plum-pudding'. Her 'superfine' one is more like the elaborate Victorian mixtures which became common as the century wore on. The 'pudding-biscuit' which she uses is simply a kind of crisp sponge biscuit made from flour, sugar and eggs; this was hardened in a cool oven, then pounded and used instead of breadcrumbs or flour.

> Take four ounces of pounded pudding-biscuit, and two ounces of the best flour or good common biscuits, a half-pound of bloom or muscatel raisins stoned, the same quantity of fresh Zante currants picked and plumped, and half a pound of suet stripped of skins and filaments, and shred; a small teaspoonful of nutmeg grated, a quarter pound of fine beat sugar, a drachm of pounded cinnamon, and two blades of mace; three ounces of candied lemon, orange and citron sliced, and two ounces of blanched almonds roughly chopped. Beat four eggs well, and put to them a little sweet milk, a glass of white wine or brandy, and mix in the flour and all the ingredients. Tie up the pudding firm, and boil it for four hours, keeping up the boil, and turning the cloth. Serve pudding sauce.

As the pudding became more elaborate, so did the sauce which went with it. At one time a little melted butter and white wine sufficed, but *The Cook's Oracle* recommends 'a glass of sherry, half a glass of brandy or curaçao, two teaspoonsful of pounded lump sugar, a little grated lemon peel and nutmeg, and a quarter of a pint of thick melted butter'. Mrs Dalgairns gives the following sauce.

> Heat two or three tablespoonfuls of sweet cream, and mix it gradually with two well-beaten yolks of eggs; add three tablespoonfuls of white wine, brandy or rum, and a tablespoonful of sugar; stir it over the fire till quite hot but do not allow it to boil.

By the middle of the nineteenth century cookery books included recipes for 'Christmas Pudding' as well as for 'Plum Pudding'. Traditionally they are supposed to be mixed on 'Stir-up Sunday'—the twenty-fifth Sunday after Trinity, i.e. last Sunday before Advent—when everyone who stirs the puddings makes a wish. Here is Eliza Acton's recipe for 'Ingoldsby Christmas Puddings'.

> Mix very thoroughly one pound of finely grated bread with the same quantity of flour, two pounds of raisins stoned, two of currants, two of suet minced small, one of sugar, half a pound of candied peel, one nutmeg, half an ounce of mixed spice, and the grated rinds of two lemons; mix the whole with sixteen eggs well beaten and strained and add four glasses of brandy. These proportions will make three puddings of good size, each of which should be boiled six hours.

Although rum or brandy butter have now replaced the old-fashioned wine sauces, the ritual of pouring brandy over the pudding is still adhered to. The Victorians loved it. 'In addition to wine sauce, have a metal sauce-boat filled with brandy; set it alight on the table, and pour a portion of it in a flame upon each slice of pudding. It will be found a great improvement.'

ABOVE LEFT
Plum puddings appeared on Christmas cards from the earliest times, usually with the traditional holly sprig and often, as on this American postcard, drawn along on a sleigh. Dated 1907, this card was one of many of the period designed in the USA, printed in Germany and distributed in Europe.

LEFT
During the Great War many silk-woven cards like this one came as Christmas greetings from soldiers to whom plum pudding and holly were part of the memories of home. On the small card inside a young girl bears a basket of mistletoe as another reminder of the season.

ABOVE
This charming card of the 1920s is in the style of the small folded cards with a cord decoration which first appeared in the 1880s. The happy children on the front of the card, however, are in strange contrast to the solemn religious verse which appears inside.

BELOW LEFT
These two little girls reflect the increasing appearance of natural-looking children on greetings cards. A production of Louis Prang, known as 'the father of the American Christmas card', this appeared in 1878 and, though not one of the 'Prize Designs' for which he later became famous, it is skilfully printed in bold colours.

RICH PLUM CAKES

The modern Christmas cake, heavy with fruit and covered with layers of marzipan and icing, seems to have had not one predecessor but several. Originally a 'marchpane' appeared at every mediaeval feast—a huge cake made entirely of the sugar and almond mixture now known as marzipan. It was lavishly decorated with sweet-meats—candied fruits and flowers—and with gold and silver leaf; often smaller versions were given as Christmas or New Year presents. Then came the 'great cakes' made from fruit, spices and wine, and appearing in early cookery books as 'plumb' or 'bride' cakes. Often these incorporated yeast, as in the following recipe of 1718 for 'A Plumb Cake'.

> Half a quarter of Flouer 3 quarters of a pound of Butter a little salt 4 eggs, half a nutmeg a little genger 3 or 4 spoonfuls of yeast 2 of Brandy 2 of white wine Mix it up with warm milk 3 quarters of a pound of currains, half a pound of Loaf sugar.

This must have turned out as a heavy, sweet currant bread rather than a rich fruit cake. But whilst such 'Common Plum Cakes' continued to be made in this way until the end of the nineteenth century, they were clearly meant either for ordinary occasions or less prosperous households. 'Bride Cakes' or 'Rich Plum Cakes', by contrast, were so heavy with fruit and nuts that they had to be made without yeast and were usually mixed with the hands. Here, from her *Art of Cookery,* are Mrs Hannah Glasse's instructions 'To Make A Rich Cake'.

> Take four pounds of flour well dried and sifted, seven pounds of currants washed and rubbed, six pounds of the best fresh butter, two pounds of Jordan almonds blanched, and beaten with orange-flower water and sack till they are fine, then take four pounds of eggs, put half the whites away, three pounds of double-refined sugar beaten and sifted, a quarter of an ounce of mace, the same of cloves and cinnamon, three large nutmegs, all beaten fine, a little ginger, half a pint of sack, half a pint of right French brandy, sweetmeats to your liking, they must be orange, lemon and citron.

Presumably 'right French Brandy' means that only the best authentic cognac should be used for such a special cake. Not only are the quantities alarming by today's standards; the method is elaborate, and necessarily so, for in the days of cooking without mechanical aids it was important to ensure thorough mixing.

> Work your butter to a cream with your hands before any of your ingredients are in, then put in your sugar and mix it well together; let your eggs be well beat and strained through a sieve, work in your almonds first, then put in your eggs, beat them all together till they look white and thick, then put in your sack, brandy and spices, shake your flour in by degrees, and when your oven is ready, put in your currants and sweetmeats as you put it in your hoop. It will take four hours baking in a quick oven. You must keep beating it with your hands all the while you are mixing of it, and when your currants are well washed and cleaned, let them be kept before the fire, so that they may go warm into your cake. This quantity will bake best in two hoops.

Whilst gingerbread and marchpane were baked in wooden moulds in a variety of shapes, fruit cakes were usually round and cooked in a 'hoop' or frame which stood upon a baking sheet. Some cooks suggest greasing the hoop with butter, others lining it with thick white paper. Often the icing was added as soon as the cake came out of the oven and it was later returned so that the sugar would harden. The following instructions are again from Mrs Glasse: 'To ice a great cake':

> Take the whites of twenty-four eggs and a pound of double-refined sugar beat and sifted fine; mix both together in a deep earthen pan, and with a wisk wisk it well for two or three hours together till it looks white and thick, then with a thin board or bunch of feathers spread it all over the top and sides of the cake; set it at a proper distance before a good clear fire, and keep turning it continually for fear of its changing colour; but a cool oven is best, and an hour will harden it. You may perfume the icing with what perfume you please.

At one time cakes as well as icings were not only flavoured but perfumed, often with marigold or gillyflower, or the popular rose-flower water. The practice of laying marzipan beneath the icing does not seem to have developed until late Victorian times, though the original marchpane was often 'frosted' with a sprinkling of sugar and rose-flower water. The following recipe for 'A Rich Plum Cake' is written next to one for marzipan which may well have been used with it. Both come from a family cookery book compiled at the end of the nineteenth century.

> Beat to a cream half a pound of salt butter and half a pound of fresh butter in a basin over a stove, then add one pound of ground sugar. Beat till white, add two eggs, beat five minutes, then another two eggs and so on till you have put in six. Take half of a pound and a half of sifted flour, from

which take a handful and shake into the mixture, then two eggs and beat for five minutes, then again a handful of flour, and so on till you have added in all twelve eggs. Have one and a half pounds of currants, cleaned, half a pound of sweet almonds blanched and cut small, one pound of orange and half a pound of citron peel cut small, half a pound of sultanas. Mix all the fruit with the remainder of the flour, then all together taking care not to beat the cake after adding fruit and flour. Pour into a prepared tin. Bake in a moderate oven nearly three hours.

It is interesting that no alcohol is added to the cake mixture. Brandy, however, is used for almond paste, composed of one pound each of ground almonds and caster sugar, mixed with two eggs beaten up with two tablespoonfuls of brandy. With or without white icing this would make an appropriate marzipan for any kind of rich fruit cake. By the turn of the century recipes for 'Christmas Cake' began to appear, though both rich and plain versions of plum cake continued to be made for some time. The decline of the festival of Twelfth Night, however, meant that its special cake, decorated with sugar figures, vanished from the culinary scene, thus ensuring the continued popularity of the cake now produced for Christmas Day.

These two colourful postcards of the early nineteen-hundreds were produced when the influence of Kate Greenaway's designs was at its height. The children above are dressed for a party in true Greenaway style, whilst those on the left are in genuine Edwardian clothes. Both cards, however, reflect the change in attitude that occurred as the Victorian era drew to a close and children were allowed to appear more natural. The heavy gilding and embossing are typical of the skilful German printing of the period.

PARTY DISHES

For grown-ups and children alike, Christmas is the time for parties and visiting. Family gatherings were particularly important to the Victorians, who regarded them as an almost sacred duty as well as a source of enjoyment. But party preparations were time-consuming, and the writers of cookery books were always aware of the need for recipes suitable for 'a cold collation' which could be prepared well in advance. Here is Eliza Acton's recipe for 'Good Chicken Patties'—always popular for supper or luncheon parties.

Raise the white flesh from a young undressed fowl, divide it once or twice, and lay it into a small clean saucepan, in which about an ounce of butter has been dissolved, and just begins to simmer; strew in a light seasoning of salt, mace and cayenne, and stew the chicken very softly indeed for about ten minutes, taking every precaution against its browning: turn into a dish with the butter and its own gravy, and let it become cold. Mince it with a good sharp knife; heat it, without allowing it to boil, in a little good white sauce (which may be made of some of the bones of the fowl), and fill ready-baked patty-crusts or small vol-au-vents with it, just before they are sent to table. Or stew the flesh only just sufficiently to render it firm, mix it after it is minced and seasoned with a spoonful of strong gravy, fill the patties, and bake them from fifteen to eighteen minutes. It is a great improvement to stew and mince a few mushrooms with the chicken.

Similar patties were made from cold turkey or game, and lobster or oyster patties were equally popular. Larger pies were also a useful standby and were often ornamented with pastry leaves or flowers to make them look festive. Pork pies in particular have always been regarded as traditionally English and in some parts of Warwickshire are still eaten for breakfast on Christmas morning. Most counties used to have their

AN ERRAND OF MERCY

"AT CHRISTMASTIDE
LET'S TUNE OUR HEARTS
TO THOUGHTS OF LOVE AND HARMONY."

own way of making these pies; Mrs Glasse gives the following recipe for 'Cheshire Pork Pye'.

> Take a loin of pork, skin it, cut it into steaks, season it with salt, nutmeg, and pepper; make a good crust, lay a layer of pork, then a large layer of pippins pared and cored, a little sugar, enough to sweeten the pye, then another layer of pork; put in half a pint of white wine, lay some butter on the top, and close your pye. If your pye be large, it will take a pint of white wine.

According to Soyer's *Modern Housewife* of 1850 a typical 'small evening party, say thirty persons', required the following bill of fare. 'In the centre, and at the head of the table, I place a large Grouse-Pie... I then on each of the wings have Fowls, Lobster Salads, Mayonnaises of Fowl, Ham, Tongue cut in slices, and dished over parsley, ornamented with Aspic Jelly; and on the sideboard I have a fine piece of Sirloin of Beef, or an Aich-bone of Beef or Fillet of Veal plain roasted... Should there be no game I have a turkey or Fowls en Galantine... or I have less poultry and add roast Pheasant, Partridges or Grouse, or a fine salad of Game.' Sixteen different puddings, and a dozen dishes of fruit and dessert biscuits completed the table which, by Victorian standards, was a model of economy and good taste.

One of the most impressive cold dishes was the 'galantine'. This was ideal at Christmas in particular. A whole turkey or capon or several smaller fowls were boned, stuffed and cooked in a rich stock which when cooled formed the jelly with which the bird was garnished. The following instructions are from Eliza Acton's *Modern Cookery*.

> Cut through the skin down the centre of the back and raise the flesh carefully on either side with the point of a sharp knife until the sockets of the wings and thighs are reached. Bone these joints; after they are once detached from it the whole body may easily be separated from the flesh and taken out entire. Fill the legs and wings with forcemeat, and the body with the livers of two or three fowls mixed with alternate layers of parboiled tongue freed from the rind, fine sausage meat, or veal forcemeat, or thin slices of the nicest bacon, or aught else of good flavour which will give a marbled appearance to the fowl when it is carved; then sew up and truss as usual.

The bird was tied up in a napkin and placed in a stewing pan as near as possible to its own size. It was simmered for two or three hours in a stock containing mixed herbs and vegetables, as well as the calves' feet and veal knuckle needed to make a good aspic jelly. Then the stock was allowed to cool, the bird removed and the liquid reduced by boiling again. As a finishing touch Alexis Soyer suggests adding 'four egg-whites whisked up in a basin with their shells, half a pint of water, two spoonfuls of tarragon or common vinegar and a glass of sherry'. These are all whisked into the stock, which is strained and cooled; the resulting jelly is cut into fancy shapes for decoration.

Family Christmas activities of all kinds are shown in this series of postcards by an English artist, Ethel Parkinson.
By the turn of the century black and muted colours were often used to good effect in card design, and the strong outlines of the figures make these examples particularly attractive.
Visiting friends and relations or those in need, and happy family reunions, were considered specially important at Christmas. The messages on these cards are clearly meant to be as meaningful as the pictures, though the total effect is nostalgic rather than moralizing.

ETHEL PARKINSON

Go where you will,
North, South, East or West,
New Friends are good,
but old Friends are best.

SNOW PUDDINGS AND YULE LOGS

Many traditional desserts are made from apples, and these are particularly welcome at Christmastime. Some dishes like apple florentine (the original apple-pie, made from layers of sliced apple, sprinkled with cider and cinnamon and covered with puff pastry) date back to Elizabethan times and were produced on all great occasions. Others were particularly favoured by Victorian cooks whose party menus often included a 'snow' of eggs and apples. The following recipe for a 'Dish of Snow, or Snow Cream', comes from *The Cook and Housewife's Manual*.

> Stew and pulp a dozen of apples; beat, and when cold stir this into the whites of a dozen eggs whipped to a strong froth; add a half-pound of sugar sifted, and the grate of a lemon. Whisk the whole together till it becomes stiff, and heap it handsomely in a glass dish.

Another 'Snow Pudding' appeared in *The Englishwoman's Domestic Magazine* for 1850, this time made from lemons. It is interesting to note the use of a patent gelatine, which for some time after it first appeared was considered much inferior to the laboriously made calves' foot or hartshorn jellies. The amount suggested here would be equivalent to two of the small three-quarter-ounce packets available today.

> Dissolve half of a sixpenny package of gelatine (Cox's we find the best) in half a pint of water; add half a pound of ground white sugar, the juice of four lemons and the whites of two eggs. Beat all up till very light and spongy, then pour into a mould. When wanted, turn into a crystal dish, and serve with a custard round it made of the yolks of two eggs.

A much more spectacular dish was the 'Hedgehog' made from whole, peeled apples heaped together and baked with a 'snow' of meringue, into which almonds or pistachios were fixed to form the spikes. A purée or 'marmalade' of several pounds of apples or apricots was needed to fill in the spaces between the whole fruit, and the preparation was so laborious that it is hardly surprising that the dish has not survived in its original form. Here is a modern version of 'Apple Hedgehog'.

> Peel and quarter two pounds of small apples and cook them gently until tender in about a quarter of a pint of water with the juice of a lemon and four ounces of sugar. When the apples are soft but not pulped, remove from heat and cool a little, then add threequarters of an ounce of gelatine previously dissolved in a little warm water, and beat in well. If available, a tablespoonful of apricot purée may be added also, or the apples coloured with a few drops of cochineal. Pour into a wetted mould and, when set, turn out and cover with thick cream and 'spikes' of sliced blanched almonds. Chill before serving.

Hot apple puddings were also popular and often these involved the favourite pastime of pouring alcohol over the pudding and serving it ablaze. For 'Apple Yule Logs', a traditional dish from the west of England, a large baking-apple is needed for each person.

> Peel and core the apples, and put them in a large baking-tin or fireproof dish. Stuff each one with mincemeat, or a mixture of chopped raisins, sugar and breadcrumbs. Mix two or three tablespoonfuls of clear honey or golden syrup with a little hot water, and pour this over the apples. Cook the apples in a warm oven until tender but not losing their shape, and whilst cooking baste them from time to time with the syrup. Remove the dish from the oven, drain off the syrup, and keep this to serve with the apples. Put the dish in a warm place, and before serving pour a little warmed rum or whisky over the centre of each apple. Then light and serve at once.

In an earlier French version, 'Pommes Flambantes' or 'Blazing Apples', the apples are poached rather than baked in a syrup and being smaller are not stuffed. When ready they are piled in a pyramid on the dish. The syrup is cooked a little longer to reduce it before being poured over the hot apples; these are then sprinkled with powdered sugar. Finally rum is poured over the pyramid and set alight. As with the individual apple yule logs, the operation is only successful if the apples are kept really hot. If properly carried out, however, it can add an element of excitement appropriate to the Christmas table.

A·Merry·Christmas·and
a·Happy·New·Year

*This folder-style card shows again the later, more
relaxed approach to children and their activities.
A small child plays at making a snow-pudding; his
companion, however, is unusually dressed as a child
Father Christmas. The sentiment inside the card
is just as simple and charming:
'I'd have thee happy as the day is long,
With Laughter, Games and Merry Song.'*

ALL
HAPPINESS AT
CHRISTMAS

*This postcard of two happy children sliding on the
ice is delicately coloured; the children's clothing
is embossed and frosted with glass frosting which
began to appear on cards during the 1880s. Such
decoration quickly became popular and lasted well
into the period after the Great War to which this
card belongs.*

THE GREAT SIR-LOIN

'This joint is said to owe its name to King Charles the Second, who dining upon a Loin of Beef, and being particularly pleased with it, asked the name of the Joint; said for its merit it should be knighted, and henceforth called Sir-Loin.' By the beginning of the nineteenth century, when Dr Kichener, writing in his *Cook's Oracle*, gave this explanation, roast beef was firmly established as the chief national dish of England. It was taken for granted that, along with plum-pudding, it would appear at Christmastime, and indeed for many poorer families this was the only time in the year that they tasted it. Though gradually superseded in importance at this season by the turkey, beef never lost its popularity and every good cook had to master the art of roasting it 'to a turn'. Here is Dr Kichener's method.

The noble Sir-Loin of about fifteen pounds, (if much thicker, the outside will be done too much before the inside is enough,) will require to be before the fire about three and a half or four hours: take care to spit it evenly, that it may not be heavier on one side than the other;—put a little clean Dripping into the dripping pan, tie a sheet of paper over it to preserve the Fat, baste it well as soon as it is put down, and every quarter of an hour all the time it is roasting, till the last half-hour; then take off the paper, and make some gravy for it, stir the fire and make it clear; to Brown and Froth it, sprinkle a little salt over it; baste it with butter, and dredge it with flour; let it go a few minutes longer, till the froth rises, take it up, put it on the dish. Garnish it with hillocks of horseradish scraped as fine as possible with a sharp knife.

Roasting a joint in this way was not only an art but something of a test of stamina. According to Kichener few cooks could cope single-handed, for 'the Spit claims exclusive attention, and is an imperious Mistress, who demands the entire devotion of her slave'. In the days when great occasions demanded the roasting of a baron of beef, which could weigh between forty and eighty pounds, the problem was partly solved by the employment of a boy as 'turnspit' whose full-time job was the turning of the spit and watching of the roast. But 'when the Cook is obliged at the same time, to attend her Fish and Soup kettles, and watch her Stewpans and all their accompaniments—if she gives that delicate and constant attention to the Roasts which is indispensably requisite, the rest of the Dinner must often be spoilt'.

Nevertheless, most cooks managed to produce the traditional Yorkshire pudding to go with the roast beef. Mrs Glasse describes how it was cooked in the old-fashioned way, in a pan below the meat.

Take a quart of milk, four eggs, and a little salt, make it up into a thick batter with flour like a pancake batter. You must have a good piece of meat at the fire, take a stew-pan and put some dripping in, set it on the fire; when it boils, pour in your pudding; let it bake on the fire till you think it is nigh enough then turn a plate upside-down in the dripping-pan, that the dripping may not be blacked; set your stew-pan on it under the meat, and let the dripping drop on the pudding, and the heat of the fire come to it, to make it of a fine brown. When your meat is done and sent to the table, drain all the fat from your pudding, and set it on the fire again to dry a little; then slide it as dry as you can into a dish, melt some butter and pour into a cup, and set in the middle of the pudding. It is an exceedingly good pudding; the gravy of the meat eats well with it.

The extra-tasty flavour was of course provided by the juices of the meat which dripped into the pudding; it is possible to achieve a similar effect during oven-roasting if the beef is placed on a grid over the pudding. But the 'Gipsies' way', as the traditional method was called, meant of course still more labour on the cook's part. So perhaps it is not surprising that a large joint of cold roasted beef or a piece of beef salted and spiced was found particularly useful at Christmas. The following method for 'Welsh Spiced Beef' is fairly simple and may be used for any large boned joint.

For ten pounds of beef take two ounces each of allspice, saltpetre and black pepper, and four ounces of salt. Rub the saltpetre well into the meat, and stand for twentyfour hours, then rub in the salt and spices mixed together. Leave the beef in an earthenware pot for a fortnight, turning each day. Then tie it round with tape and put it in a baking-pan; pour melted suet over, then cover the pan with flour and water paste. Bake in a slow oven for twelve hours. Remove the crust, and press the beef between two plates with a weight on top for several hours.

Cold beef prepared in this way will keep for several weeks and is particularly good if stuffed with sweet herbs before baking. For occasions when the roast sirloin was too laborious a dish spiced beef was an acceptable substitute, and it became a firm favourite in Victorian and Edwardian households, especially at times like Christmas when large numbers of visitors were expected.

Friendship is the theme of these folder cards of the 1880s.
The designs show increasing sophistication as well as
interesting use of the traditional Christmas
red and green.

From the firm of W. McKenzie, the meeting between Holly and
Mistletoe reflects the sentiment printed inside the card:
'Times alter as the years go past —
What matter so our friendships last.'

The trimming is a simple coloured cord, typical of this
period of card design.

Although the lady golfer is obviously emancipated, inside
this card with its fashionable ribbon trim is an old-fashioned
verse. The author, Constance Dubois, was one of many women
who found writing 'sentiments' a useful way of making money.
'Remembrance.
I send you this to forge anew,
The links of friendship's chain,
And bear my wishes warm, that you
Much joy from Christmas gain.'

MULLED DRINKS

Hot spiced wines, and ale or spirits 'hotted up' were at one time an essential part of the winter festival. Eggs, cream and spices were all popular additions, and the earliest recipes like 'hippocras'—wine sweetened and seasoned with aromatic spices—or 'clary'—claret mixed with honey and spice—were drunk not only at banquets but also as medicine or nightcaps. Indeed any occasion could be made an excuse for enjoying these beverages, one of which—'bishop'—remained in use through Victorian times. Eliza Acton gives the 'Oxford Recipe for Bishop'.

Make several incisions in the rind of a lemon, stick cloves in these, and roast the lemon by a slow fire. Put small but equal quantities of cinnamon, cloves, mace and allspice with a trace of ginger, into a saucepan with half a pint of water: let it boil until it is reduced by one half. Boil one bottle of port wine, burn a portion of the spirit out of it by applying a lighted paper to the saucepan; put the roasted lemon and spice into the wine; stir it up well, and let it stand near the fire ten minutes. Rub a few knobs of sugar on the rind of the lemon, put the sugar into a bowl or jug, with the juice of half a lemon (not roasted), pour the wine into it, grate in some nutmeg, sweeten it to the taste, and serve it up with the lemon and spice floating in it.

If root ginger is not available ground ginger may be substituted, and a Seville orange roasted instead of the lemon is considered by some to have an 'infinitely finer flavour'. Eliza Acton's comment is borne out by Mrs Dalgairns's recipe for bishop, made this time not from port but from claret—now probably a more practicable recipe.

Roast four good-sized bitter oranges till they are of a pale brown colour; lay them in a tureen, and put over them half a pound of pounded loaf sugar, and three glassfuls of claret; place the cover on the tureen, and let it stand till next day. When required for use, put the tureen into a pan of boiling water, press the oranges with a spoon, and run the juice through a sieve; then boil the remainder of the bottle of claret, taking care that it do not burn; add to it the strained juice, and serve it warm in glasses.

In contrast to the precise instructions of the cookery books, the recipes for mulls which appear in personal notebooks tend to be delightfully vague. Here is one for a hot 'Punch' dated 1895.

A score of lemons cut in half and squeezed; three or four pounds of sugar, a kettle of boiling water, six bottles of claret, three of sherry, one gallon of whisky, then taste and see what is wanted.

A more common addition to this kind of punch was curaçao. Usually, however, hot wine punches or mulls seem to acquire their heady flavour from the addition of aromatics, whilst drinks using spirits are nearly always made smoother by the addition of eggs, milk or cream. Then all the spice that is needed is a sprinkling of nutmeg or cinnamon, as in the following recipe for 'Auld Man's Milk', which comes from Meg Dods.

Beat the yolks and whites of six eggs separately. Put to the beat yolks a quart of new milk, or thin sweet cream. Add to this rum, whisky or brandy, to taste (about a half-pint). Slip in the whipped whites, and give the whole a gentle stir up in the china punch-bowl, in which it should be mixed. It may be flavoured with nutmeg or lemon-zest.

It seems as though the punch-bowl must have been in constant use throughout the old-fashioned Christmas. English 'wassail-cups' of spiced ale with cream and apples were produced in particular on Christmas Eve, at New Year and for the celebration of Twelfth Night. In Scotland, however, Hogmanay was marked by the making of what Meg Dods called 'the national beverage'. This was the famous 'Het Pint', which was made in the following manner.

Grate a nutmeg into two quarts of mild ale, and bring it to the point of boiling. Mix a little cold ale with a considerable quantity of sugar and three eggs well beaten. Gradually mix the hot ale with the eggs, taking care that they do not curdle. Put in a half-pint of whisky, and bring it once more nearly to the boil, and then briskly pour it from one vessel into another till it becomes smooth and bright. This beverage, carried round in a bright copper tea-kettle, is the celebrated New-Year's morning 'Het Pint' of Edinburgh and Glasgow. In Aberdeen, half-boiled sowens is used on the same festive occasion. A more refined composition is made substituting white wine for ale, and brandy for whisky.

The picture conjured up by Mrs Dods of bright, steaming kettles being taken from house to house in the early hours of the morning by groups of cheerful wassailers seems to epitomize the traditional New Year spirit.

Herzlichen Glückwunsch
ZUM NEUEN JAHRE

Traditionally the chimney-sweep is a lucky visitor at New Year,
when a dark-haired man should be the first to cross the
threshold; presumably being black with soot all over the
sweep is considered to bring more luck than most. This German
postcard shows him bearing a bottle and surrounded with
snow — a distinctly seasonal figure. Though the colours are
muted, the message embossed in gold adds a festive note in a
style typical of the early nineteen-hundreds.

HOGMANAY BUN

The Scottish 'Black Bun' which is served to first-footing callers at Hogmanay was at one time a Twelfth Night Cake. But the Protestant reformers frowned upon the festivities of this day, as upon so much else to do with the Christmas season, and so the famous Bun became part of the New Year celebration. It was one of the earliest fruit cakes, appearing as 'A Rich Bun' in Mrs MacIver's *Cookery and Pastry* in the mid-eighteenth century. It was distinguished from other rich cakes, even as early as this, by its case made of yeast dough which was wrapped all round the filling of flour, fruit and spices. Mrs Dalgairns's instructions for 'Scots Christmas Bun' were written more than half a century after Mrs MacIver's recipe, but the two are almost identical.

> Take four pounds of raisins stoned, two and a half of currants well cleaned and dried, half a pound of almonds blanched, of candied orange and lemon peel a quarter of a pound of each, cut small; of pounded cloves, Jamaica pepper, and ginger, half an ounce each, four pounds of flour, and twenty-two ounces of butter. Then rub the butter with the flour, till well mixed together; add a little warm water, and a quarter of a pint of fresh good yeast, and work it into a light smooth paste; cut off nearly one-third of the paste, to form the sheet or case, and lay it aside; with the rest work up the fruit, sweetmeats, and spices; make it into a round form like a thick cheese. Roll out the sheet of paste, lay the bun in the centre, and gather it all round, closing it at the bottom, by wetting the edges of the paste, and cutting it so as to lie quite flat. Turn it up, and run a wire or small skewer through from the top to the bottom every here and there, and prick the top with a fork. Double and flour a sheet of grey paper, and lay the bun upon it; bind a piece round the sides, also doubled and floured, to keep the bun in a proper shape. Bake it in a moderate oven.

Nowadays the bun is usually made in a square shape rather than the rounded 'cheese' shape suggested by Mrs Dalgairns, and it is often baked months in advance. 'Jamaica' pepper is in fact allspice, but some cooks prefer to use black pepper; this gives the bun a really spicy flavour which is specially welcome in cold weather. Rum or brandy is often added in place of some of the milk and makes the mixture suitably festive. Here is a modern version which uses baking powder instead of yeast.

> Make a firm dough using half a pound of flour, mixed with half a teaspoonful of baking-powder; four ounces of butter; a little water. Line a large, greased cake tin with the pastry, thinly rolled out, and reserve some dough for the top. For the filling, take one pound of flour, twelve ounces of raisins, four ounces each of blanched almonds, currants and chopped mixed peel, eight ounces of soft brown sugar, two teaspoonfuls of black pepper. Mix all well together using a large cup of milk, and rum to taste. Place all in the lined tin, wet the edges of the pastry lining and cover with a pastry lid. Make sure the bun is securely pinched together, brush the top with beaten egg, prick with a fork, make several skewer holes right through to the bottom of the bun. Bake in a moderate oven for about four hours.

The Welsh too have their special New Year loaf—'bara brith' or 'speckled bread'—which is similar to the English 'spiced bread'. Traditionally the dark-haired stranger who 'first-foots' the household is given a slice of this with a mug of hot ale. The following recipe is an old-fashioned one and will make two good-sized loaves.

> Take three pounds of flour, a pint and a half of warm milk and water, and three-quarters of an ounce of yeast. Mix a dough in the usual way, and set in a warm place until well risen. Melt eight ounces of lard until warm, not hot, and mix thoroughly into the dough. Then work in eight ounces each of raisins, currants, sultanas and sugar, with two ounces of candied peel. Add half an ounce of mixed spice, then three well-beaten eggs. Knead all well together and place in greased loaf tins. Allow to rise, then bake in a hot oven for about an hour.

The New Year loaves of Wales are not made to the same enormous size as the Scottish bun, which in earlier times often weighed as much as twenty or thirty pounds. But they are essentially part of the same ancient tradition—that of welcoming the young year with seeds and fruits which symbolize its renewed promise of abundance to come.

The custom of sending special New Year messages, which dates back to ancient times, survived despite the nineteenth-century fashion for Christmas cards. Small cards, which like the early Christmas greetings card were often little larger than visiting-cards, often carried separate New Year wishes or verses, though the design sometimes included Christmas motifs like robins and snow.

This scrap card has decorative deckle edges and an unusual border of ivy leaves and holly berries round the glued-on picture of a stage-coach stopping at a country inn.

The robins ringing in the New Year, surrounded by a bold line border, are colourful and unusual.

The popular tradition of first-footing is referred to in the words printed beneath the messenger-boy, 'Welcome, little stranger!'

BANNOCKS AND GOD-CAKES

At one time New Year's Day was the day for giving and receiving gifts. Some of these were reminders of continuing goodwill and fruitfulness—an orange stuck with cloves, a gingerbread cake, or some apples. Others were more sophisticated, like the gloves and pins which were much prized by ladies in Elizabethan times, or the clothes, jewels and bales of cloth which Queen Elizabeth herself received from her subjects, anxious to show their loyalty and win her favour.

The 'god-cakes' of Coventry and its neighbourhood are also part of an earlier tradition—that of giving small cakes as gifts outside churches on festival days. On New Year's Day godparents presented their godchildren with special cakes, triangular in shape to symbolize the Trinity and made of rich pastry filled with mincemeat. Like so many dishes of ancient origin they are rarely mentioned in cookery books, but one writer describes them, in the year 1902, as still being 'produced at all prices from a penny to a guinea'. A version of god-cakes also appears in a book of popular recipes of this period as 'New Year Cakes', which are described as 'more digestible than mincepies'. Here is the recipe; no mention is made of their shape, but they would probably be made from squares of pastry folded over to form triangles.

> Take equal weight of chopped apples and raisins, brown sugar, candied peel and currants. To one pound of mixture put the juice and rind of one lemon, and half a teaspoonful of mixed spice. Make into small cakes with flaky paste, and brush over with white of egg and sprinkle sugar over.

The Christmas god-cakes or 'kitchels' of Suffolk are still made, in similar fashion to those of Coventry, with a filling of fruit and almonds spiced with nutmeg and cinnamon and encased in puff pastry. But the custom of giving these cakes has largely died out, whereas that of providing slices of cake or fruit loaf for children who come 'a-wassailing' continues in many places. Sometimes adults too still go round the neighbourhood 'guising' or 'mumming', and a gift for the 'guisers' is essential. Shortbread is usually given in Scotland but at one time 'farls' of oatmeal bannock—to be eaten with cheese—were the expected reward. These bannocks are often made today by the method Mrs Dalgairns recommended in the early nineteenth century. If preferred, however, a small knob of butter or lard may be rubbed into the meal, and some people find it easier to mix them with hot rather than cold water.

> One only should be made at a time, as the mixture dries quickly. Put two or three handfuls of meal into a bowl, and moisten it with water merely sufficient to form into a cake; knead it out round and round with the hands upon a paste-board, strewing meal under and over it; it may be made as thin as a wafer, or thicker according to taste, and put it on a hot plate called a girdle. Bake it till it be a little brown on the under side, then take it off and toast that side before the fire which was uppermost on the girdle. To make these cakes soft, they must not be toasted before the fire but both sides done quickly on the girdle.

A heavy frying pan makes a satisfactory substitute for the girdle and if wished the cakes may be cut into the more familiar 'farls' or wedge shapes before being baked.

One of the most popular New Year presents from Scotland is the 'Selkirk Bannock'. Since the 1850s large quantities have been made by bakers in the town, and they are dispatched to all parts of the world. Like bara brith the Selkirk bannock is a yeast loaf, but it is distinguished by its flavour of butter and its lack of spices.

> Make a bread dough using one pound of flour, one ounce of fresh yeast; mix with four ounces of butter or lard melted and added to half a pint of warm milk. Allow the dough to rise in a warm place, then knead in four ounces of caster sugar, half a pound of cleaned currants and sultanas, and two ounces of chopped candied peel. When well mixed, form into a round and place in a greased round tin. Rise for about half an hour, then bake until light brown. Glaze with a sugar and water mixture on removing from the oven, after about an hour's baking.

This bannock was a favourite of Queen Victoria, and like the black bun was sometimes made to a great size. Since it keeps well it can be made before Christmas and, being so rich, can serve a good many guests when produced at a New Year gathering.

WITH BEST WISHES FOR A HAPPY CHRISTMAS.

WISHING YOU A BRIGHT AND HAPPY CHRISTMAS.

These unusual small cards of the 1880s were probably intended to accompany gifts for Christmas and New Year. The delicate designs are reminiscent of earlier engravings of country scenes, though their simplicity is offset by the two bands of gold which encircle them. The tiny figures of a man gathering wood and a woman beside a water-mill are surrounded by snow and leafless trees on the two cards intended for Christmas, while appropriate spring-like landscapes appear on the two New Year cards.

LOVE. JOY. PEACE CROWN THY NEW YEAR.

WISHING YOU A HAPPY NEW YEAR.

HAGGIS AND MUTTON-PIES

'Great chieftain o' the puddin'-race!' was the poet Burns's description of the Scottish 'Haggis', and it was in this superior capacity that the dish appeared at all important feasts including that of Hogmanay. It was one of the earliest of 'bag-puddings'—after all, the sheep's stomach made an ideal receptacle for cooking the animal's 'pluck', as its liver and heart and lights are known. Suet, onions and oatmeal also formed part of the original pudding and as it became more elaborate eggs and spices were sometimes added too. In 1777 Mrs MacIver gave two recipes, one for 'A Good Scots Haggies' on which many future cooks based their versions of the dish, and another for a 'Lamb's Haggies' as follows.

Clean the bag very well; slit up all the little fat tripes and the rodikin with a pair of scissors, and wash them very clean; parboil them, and what kernals you can get about the lamb; then cut in little pieces, but not too small; shred the web very small, and mix it with the other cut meat, and season it properly with a little salt and spices; cast three eggs with three spoonfuls of flour, as for pancake batter; mix them up with a mutchkin of sweet milk; have a handful of young parsley and some chives, or young onions, shred very small; then mix all the materials very well into the batter; put all into the bag, and sew it up; it will take about an hour's boiling.

In spite of the use of a batter instead of suet and stock for mixing, it is clear at once that the method of preparing a haggis has changed little down the centuries. The instructions which follow are taken from a book of traditional recipes collected after the First World War.

Well clean the haggis bag and boil the sheep's head and liver, chop it up finely. Finely shred one pound of suet and chop up small a pound of onions. Add half a pound of oatmeal, season well with salt, pepper and ground spice. Put the mixture in the bag to about half full, add about a pint of the stock from the head and liver; then sew up the bag, pressing out the air as you do so. Boil gently for about three hours, occasionally pricking the bag with a needle to prevent it from bursting.

This highly elaborate New Year card combines all the decorative elements that seem to have appealed to the Victorians, whatever the occasion. Three sections are encased in frames of silver paper lace, and hinged together with strips of silk. The woven silk centre by Thomas Stevens of Coventry is padded with green tissue and shows an embroidered robin with a greeting below –
'A happy year, a happy year,
may this just entered be!
A happy, sunny, peaceful year
Be granted thine and thee!'

To left and right of the robin satin panels support flower 'scraps', with a larger flower picture and a faintly biblical scene on the reverse. Behind the centre panel is an oval satin pad printed with a second New Year message. Whether a manufactured or, as seems more likely, a home-made card, this is a well-preserved example of Victorian taste and ingenuity,

The Scottish tradition of plain haggis continued, whilst the English version became much more elaborate during the nineteenth century. Spices, wine and even dried fruit were added in deference to the Victorian taste for sweet dishes. Here is Richard Dolby's recipe from his *Cook's Dictionary*.

Take the heart and the lights from a sheep, blanch and mince them; then a pound of beef-suet (chopped fine), the crumb of a French Roll soaked in cream, a little mace, nutmeg, cinnamon, and cloves, (all pounded), half a pint of sweet wine, a pound of raisins, stoned and chopped, a sufficient quantity of flour to make it of a proper consistence, a little salt, the yolks of three eggs, and some sheep's chitterlings well cleaned and cut into slips. Mix these together; have ready cleaned a sheep's bag, put in the above, tie it tight, and boil it three hours.

Another Scottish speciality, the great mutton-pie, made from 'handsome mutton chops' was also much to the Victorian taste. The Queen herself ordered smaller mutton patties to be served regularly at her Balmoral receptions. But 'sweet mutton pies' were also part of English Christmas tradition. Rum was added and the pastry was usually rich with butter. This is a recipe for a large pie.

Cut the meat from a pound of fat mutton chops into half-inch squares. Mix together half a pound each of currants, raisins and sultanas, with six ounces of soft brown sugar and four ounces of candied peel. Put the meat and fruit in alternate layers in a large pie-dish, seasoning each layer with cinnamon, nutmeg, mace, and a little pepper and salt. Finally pour over two wineglassfuls of rum, and the juice of a large lemon. Cover the pie with puff pastry and bake in a very hot oven until well browned. Reduce to moderate heat after the first fifteen minutes to enable the meat and fruit to cook well.

In Yorkshire and Cumberland farmhouses these were often served instead of the more usual plum-pudding. 'Rum and Mutton pies' are still often made between Boxing Day and New Year's Day and, like the better-known haggis, they show how an ancient regional dish can survive the centuries as an unchanging part of the great Christmas festival.

BALMORAL MENU

During her frequent visits to Balmoral Queen Victoria adopted a half English, half Scottish cuisine which became the norm for the establishments of English gentry who spent many weeks of the year on their estates in Scotland. Many of the Balmoral dishes were specially suited to the Christmas season when there was plenty of venison and game. Some were adaptations of traditional Scots delicacies; others were imported, along with the Queen's household, from Windsor. Amongst these was 'Queen Victoria Soup', created by the Esquire of Windsor Kitchen in 1842 and based on an old recipe from the court of James V of Scotland.

> Skin and entirely clean out the insides of three fat fowls. Stew these for an hour in a good veal broth, with plenty of parsley. When soft, take out the fowls and soak in the broth the crums of two French rolls. Remove the flesh from the fowls and pound it in a mortar with the soaked bread and the yolks of four hard-boiled eggs. Press through a sieve and add a quart of previously boiled cream. Season lightly and re-heat gently before serving.

At Christmas and New Year particularly, venison formed part of the main course in more well-to-do households. Whether roasted in the traditional way or baked in a 'huff paste' in the same manner as ham, venison was usually served with a piquant sauce of 'currant jelly melted in red wine' according to Meg Dods. Here are her instructions 'To roasting Red Deer or Roe'.

> Season the haunch highly, by rubbing it well with mixed spices. Soak it for six hours in claret, and a quarter pint of the best vinegar, or the fresh juice of three lemons, turn it frequently, and baste with the liquor. Strain the liquor in which the venison was soaked; add to it fresh butter melted, and with this baste the haunch during the whole time it is roasting. Fifteen minutes before the roast is drawn, remove the paper, and froth and brown with flour as for other roasts.

The 'paper' mentioned here is the buttered paper with which venison, being a notoriously dry meat, is covered whilst roasting. Sometimes the paper was itself covered with a layer of thin flour and water paste which, like that used for baking joints, helped still further to retain the juices and protect the flesh. The natural toughness of much of the venison resulted in the development of dishes which used up surplus meat. Pies and patties of course were popular and so too was 'Hashed Venison'. Here is a recipe which originated in the Balmoral kitchens.

> Add a few peppercorns to a wineglassful of vinegar, and heat until reduced to about threequarters. Add to this some brown sauce, and some gravy made from the venison bones and trimmings, and boil for a few minutes. Add one spoonful of either red-currant or cranberry jelly. Strain, then mix with the finely-hashed venison, and simmer gently till well-heated.

Boiled puddings were much favoured in the Queen's kitchen to judge by the numerous titles given to these puddings during the nineteenth century—including 'Her Majesty's', 'Prince Regent's' and even 'Royal Nursery' puddings. But when in Scotland Victoria enjoyed the native 'cream' desserts which came to be much in evidence as alternatives to plum-pudding at Christmas. 'Caledonian cream' is one with a long history, and which has survived to the present day.

> To one pint of thick cream add the following: one dessertspoonful of finely minced marmalade, one table-spoonful of brandy, the juice of half a lemon, and sifted sugar to taste. Whisk until the cream is well thickened, and serve chilled in a glass bowl.

Along with such desserts it was customary to serve sweet biscuits or small cakes, and often these were of the sponge or shortcake kind. The following recipe appeared in later cookery-books as 'Holyrood Rout Cakes', but in fact had its origin in earlier times when, during the eighteenth century in particular, 'rout cakes' were perhaps the most popular of all small biscuit-cakes. Here is Mrs Dods's early nineteenth-century version.

> To the beat yolks of twelve eggs put half a pound of butter beat to a cream, half a pound of sifted sugar, the fresh grate of a lemon, and twelve ounces of flour dried. Season this with a little orange-flower water, or a few pounded almonds. When very well mixed, pour the cake into a paper mould. Let it be scarcely an inch thick, bake it and when cool ice it, and cut it with a sharp knife and ruler into squares, lozenges, diamonds, &c. Moisten the edges of these bits with sugar, and crisp them before the fire.

These small decorated cakes were, of course, suitable for children's parties as well as for adult gatherings. Under Victoria the family Christmas flourished, and the preservation of such old-fashioned confections was only one aspect of the nostalgia for the past that became increasingly evident as the century wore on.

I WISH YOU A HAPPY NEW YEAR.

BUDS AND BLOSSOMS STREW THY PATH.

ABOVE
*Though not printed as such on the reverse,
this card of about 1880 has the size and shape of a
conventional postcard. Perhaps Queen Victoria's
love of Scotland influenced the designer, though
his kilted huntsmen, and horse laden with deer and
pheasant, have a rather mediaeval air. The colours
are skilfully printed and the scene is
bordered with a fine gold line.*

LEFT
*Here the 'Japanese' theme is highly sentimental,
though it reflects a genuine interest in China and
Japan during the 1880s. The greeting 'Buds and Blossoms
strew thy Path', and the almond blossom design are
typical of the Victorian association of spring
flowers with the New Year. The card has a
heavy silver border and silver is also printed on
the branches of the tree.*

GAME

Shoots, deer-stalking and hunt meets are all part of the New Year's activities. The provision of game for the Victorian table meant such welcome additions to the menu as game soup, terrine or salmi of pheasant and hare, and even, for breakfast, grouse on toast. Here are Mrs Rundell's recommendations for 'Hunter's Soup'.

When sportsmen bivouac upon the moor, the produce of the game-bag must be put into the soup-kettle with any odds and ends of other meat, and a bottle or two of any wine or beer that can be spared; then filling it with water commence the brew, which must be intrusted to any servant, he being only required to begin early in the morning, and let the game stew long enough to extract from it the entire of its juices. When the party returns in the evening from shooting they will thus find the essential requisite of a good soup.

The resulting stock could be used in a variety of ways; whether providing the basis of a special sauce or a soup, the maintenance of the stock-pot was sound economy and the results of the cook's labours often delicious. The following is Mrs Rundell's 'Game Soup'.

Take any portion of white meat that is left (from a roast for example), and pound it in a mortar. Put the backs and legs in a stewpan with a pint of veal gravy (or other stock) and a slice of lean ham, two or three green onions, pepper, and salt. Stew till all the goodness is extracted, then take out the backs and legs and put in a pint of strong gravy; take the yolks of two hard-boiled eggs and pound them with the meat that is in the mortar; rub it through a sieve and add to the liquor. Season very moderately as it ought to possess the high game flavour.

Ideal for a cold January night, such soup might be followed by a number of supper dishes including the following 'Terrine of Hare'. Hare dishes of all kinds were popular as part of the Victorian family menu and often feature upon the Christmas bills of fare in cookery books.

Cut the flesh from a hare, and slice it into neat fillets. Have ready some stuffing and some fresh sausage meat with some sliced bacon. Put a layer of stuffing at the bottom of the terrine, and lay on this thin slices of bacon, then a layer of hare, and lastly a slice of sausage meat, repeating these layers till the terrine is full, seasoning each with pepper, spice, etc, and sprinkling them with sherry or port wine, and some good stock made from the carcase of the hare. When full lay a slice of raw bacon on the top cover with a buttered paper, and bake in a moderate oven for one to one and a half hours.

Ways of dishing up hare and the commoner game birds are included in most Victorian cookery books, and skill in dealing with them was necessary for any good housekeeper. The French chef Soyer mentions, however, in his mid-century *Modern Housewife* some unfamiliar varieties of bird. The 'White Grouse or Ptarmigan' and the 'Red-breasted Shoveller, which we receive in London from Holland about Christmas' are only two of the many which assiduous tradesmen managed to procure for the tables of the rich. Meanwhile, in the country, the Boxing Day or New Year shoot produced the more familiar pheasant or grouse for the overworked cook to transform into dishes like the following 'Pheasant Stewed with Cabbage' recommended by Soyer himself—'an excellent method for dressing a pheasant which should prove to be rather old, though a young one would be preferable'.

> Procure a large savoy, which cut into quarters, and well wash in salt and water, after which boil it five minutes in plain water, then drain it quite dry, cut off the stalk, season rather highly with pepper and salt. Have ready a middling size onion, and half a pound of streaky bacon, which with the cabbage put into a stewpan, covering the whole with a little good broth. Let it simmer at the corner of the fire three-quarters of an hour, then thrust the pheasant (previously three parts roasted) into the cabbage, and let them stew three-quarters of an hour longer, or until the stock has reduced to glaze and adheres thickly to the cabbage. Dress the cabbage in a mound upon your dish, with the bacon cut into slices around, and the pheasant upon the top, half way buried in the cabbage. Have a little game sauce, which pour round and serve.

The ubiquitous stock-pot, of course, once again proved invaluable for this, as for so many game dishes. With sportsmen only too willing to forsake for a few hours the holly-decked rooms and cheerful fireside, and numerous guests and large families ready to consume enormous meals, it is no wonder that such recipes abound in the family cookery books of the Victorians.

This is a delightful example of a typical 'animated' card of the 1870s, when the Victorian penchant for complicated surprise cards was at its height. At first sight a conventional floral greeting upon an elaborately gilded card, it is in fact composed of a series of scraps slotted into the background with ribbons. When a ribbon hidden at the top of the card is pulled the bouquet opens downwards to reveal a series of New Year messages fixed to the back of each scrap, set against a background of tiny figures in a variety of happy scenes – children fishing and boating, a family out walking. Apart from some damage to the greeting at the bottom, this is a well-preserved card still in perfect working order.

THE WASSAIL-BOWL

'Lambs-wool', the traditional Old English wassail drink, was originally the speciality of Twelfth-Eve, January 5th. This was the night when in many counties of England the apple-trees in the orchards were ceremoniously 'wassailed' to ensure a good crop for the year to come. Sometimes the custom took place on Christmas Eve or on December 31st and in one or two places at Candlemas, which once marked the end of Yule-tide; but for the most part it came as part of the Twelfth-tide celebrations.

The 'wassail bowl' itself contained a mixture of ale, sugar, nutmeg and roasted apples and this steaming mixture was carried from house to house or passed round the assembled company. Here is the modern version of this ancient concoction.

Take half a dozen large cooking apples, or about two pounds of crab apples, and bake or poach them whole until the skins are soft. Remove the skins and cores and mash the pulp in a large bowl. Heat slowly, until steaming well, two pints of ale and one of sweet wine, or three pints of draught cider if preferred. Before heating add to the ale or cider a stick of cinnamon or half a teaspoonful of ground cinnamon, along with a teaspoonful of grated nutmeg, and a sprinkling of ground ginger. When heated

remove the cinnamon stick and pour the mixture over the mashed apples. Stir in soft brown sugar to taste, and strain all through a sieve, pressing the pulp through. Reheat and serve in a large bowl or in mugs.

In the west of England another kind of wassail drink was known as 'Egg-hot', being made of cider heated and mixed with spices and beaten eggs. Apples were hung on strings and roasted in the fireplace, then dropped sizzling into the wassail-bowl. When all the eating and drinking was over the farmer and his men carried the bowl out to the orchard, where cider and pieces of apple were poured over the roots of the best apple-tree. In some places it is still the custom to go out and drink toasts to the trees whilst shots are fired through the branches.

Health to thee, good apple-tree,
Well to bear, pocket-fulls, hat-fulls,
Peck-fulls, bushel-bag-fulls.

Sometimes pieces of toasted bread dipped in cider were placed in the branches of the tree and often spiced bread or cakes were dipped into the wassail drink. The caraways or other seeds in the bread were

With their appealing blend of ingenuity and simplicity, these small cards are typical mid-Victorian productions.

Mounted on a visiting-card with paper-lace edges, this card of 1866 has a hinged foreground to which the figures of father and children, in their formal dress, are attached. Wreaths of holly and ivy surround the snow-covered cottage with its cut-out window through which Mama watches her family depart on their Christmas outing.

This curious New Year figure seems to be a mixture of Old Father Time and a court jester. 'Guisers' and other traditional wassailers often featured on early greetings cards: this one is perhaps intended to represent the original 'Father Christmas'. He sometimes appeared among the mummers who once provided Yuletide entertainment in great houses.

supposed to represent the next year's harvest, and in Scotland shortbread sprinkled with caraways was eaten on Twelfth Eve as well as at other festivals.

Whilst the traditional 'lambs-wool' continued to be made in the countryside, a more refined version found its way into Victorian cookery books and on to the dining-table. Meg Dods observes that 'A very good wassail-bowl may be made of mild ale well spiced and sweetened and a plain rice-custard with a few eggs'. She also gives the following recipe for 'Wassail-Bowl, a Centre Supper-dish'.

> Crumble down as for Trifle a nice fresh cake (or use maccaroons or other small biscuits) into a china punch-bowl or deep glass dish. Over this pour some sweet rich wine, as Malmsey Madeira, if wanted very rich, but raisin wine will do. Sweeten this, and pour a well-seasoned rich custard over it, and stick it over with sliced blanched almonds. This is in fact just a rich eating-posset.

'Possets' of all kinds had been popular from Elizabethan times, and they varied from the simpler kinds used to treat colds and other ailments to richer ones consumed at weddings and other festivals. Like 'lambs-wool' some had a base of heated ale or cider and others were made from sack or sherry. Mrs Glasse

gives three recipes, including the following 'To make an excellent Sack Posset' in which she describes the traditional method of mixing a posset.

> Beat fifteen eggs, whites and yolks very well, and strain them; then put three quarters of a pound of white sugar into a pint of canary, and mix it with your eggs in a basin; set it over a chaffing-dish of coals, and keep continually stirring it till it is scalding hot. In the meantime grate some nutmeg into a quart of milk, and boil it; then pour into your eggs and wine, they being scalded hot. Hold your hand very high as you pour it, and somebody stirring it all the time you are pouring in the milk: then take it off the chaffing-dish, set it before the fire half an hour, and serve it up.

Whether for eating or for drinking, possets were clearly suitable for convivial occasions of all kinds and it is hardly surprising that the wassail-bowl became a symbol of Christmas cheer and fellowship. The following description comes from *The Gentleman's Magazine* of 1784.

> And after supper was brought in the wassail cup or wassail bowl, of which every one partook, by taking with a spoon, out of the ale, a roasted apple, and eating it, and then drinking the healths of the company out of the bowl, wishing them a merry Christmas and a happy new year.

This unusual bell-shaped card probably dates from the 1880s. The snowy scene, with its tiny figures on their way to church, is lightly frosted with silver, while the New Year message appears at the base of the 'bell'.

An early Raphael Tuck design, this card shows the increasing technical skill of the card manufacturers. The mock visiting-card bears a gilded greeting, with the cut-out 'Good Luck' above also in gold, and the holly decoration is heavily embossed.

TWELFTH CAKE

'Scarcely a shop in London that offers a halfpenny plain bun to a hungry boy, is without Twelfth-cakes and finery in the windows on Twelfth-day.' William Hone compiling his *Every-day Book* of 1826 described the customs of the Twelfth-tide festival, little knowing that before the turn of the nineteenth century the games and ceremonies would almost be forgotten and that recipes for the special cakes would no longer appear in cookery books.

One of the few places where the celebration was continued was the Drury Lane Theatre, where the traditional cake with its lucky bean at the centre is served with port wine negus, in memory of Robert Baddeley, an eighteenth-century actor and chef. Here is a recipe for 'Twelfth Cake' from *The Cook's Oracle,* compiled not long after Baddeley's death in 1794.

Two pounds of sifted Flour, two pounds of sifted Loaf Sugar, two pounds of Butter, eighteen Eggs, four pounds of Currants, one half pound Almonds, blanched and chopped, one half pound Citron, one pound of Candied Orange and Lemon Peel, cut into thin slices, a large Nutmeg grated, half an ounce ground Allspice; ground Cinnamon, Mace, Ginger, and Corianders, a quarter of an ounce of each, and a gill of Brandy.

Put the Butter into a stewpan, in a warm place, and work it into a smooth cream with the hand, and mix it with the Sugar and Spice in a pan (or on your paste board), for some time; then break in the Eggs by degrees, and beat it at least twenty minutes;—stir in the Brandy, and then the Flour, and work it a little—add the Fruit, Sweetmeats, and Almonds, and mix all together lightly,—have ready a hoop cased with paper, on a baking plate,—put in the mixture, smooth it on the top with your hand—dipped in milk—put the plate on another, with sawdust between, to prevent the bottom from colouring too much,—bake it in a slow oven four hours or more, and when nearly cold, ice it.

According to Hone, the cakes which appeared in shop windows 'were of all sizes and prices, and decorated with all imaginable images of things animate and inanimate. Stars, castles, kings, cottages, dragons, trees, fish, palaces, cats, dogs, churches, lions, milkmaids, knights, serpents, painted with variegated colours.' But most popular of all were the little figures of the Three Kings; for Epiphany, January 6th, was their festival. In parts of France a special cake is still made for this occasion with china figures of the kings hidden in the centre, whilst other places make smaller round 'galettes des rois' to be eaten with wine or beer on Twelfth Eve. In his *Biscuit-baker's and Pastrycook's Assistant,* Thomas Shoesmith tells his readers to 'lay on your ornaments while the icing is wet. You may get the ornaments from the wholesale confectioners.' Here are his instructions for 'Twelfth Cake'.

Prepare your mixture as for bride-cake, plum-cake, or pound-cake, which you please: if you prepare it as for pound-cake, take two pounds of currants, and four ounces of candied orange and lemon-peel, to every pound of sugar. Take one pound of butter, beat it with your hand in a warm pan until it comes to a fine cream; put in one pound of powdered loaf sugar, beat it together to a nice cream; have one pound and a quarter of flour sifted, put in a little, and give it a stir; put in four eggs, beat it well; then take a little more flour and four more eggs as before, and beat it well again; then stir in the remainder of your flour. If you bake them in small cakes, butter the tins; if in large cakes, paper the tins: sugar over the top, and bake in a moderate heat.

Caster sugar may be substituted for the powdered loaf sugar used here. The fruit would be added last of all, and the final sprinkling of sugar is only needed if the cakes are not to be iced.

It was Mary Queen of Scots who brought to her court in Scotland the French custom of the 'gâteau des rois'—'cake of the Kings'—and the 'Feast of the Bean'. From then on during the English festivities, a bean, and sometimes a pea, would be hidden in the cake and the lucky recipients were designated King or Queen of the feast. Often at Twelfth-night parties the other guests were given tickets bearing the names of a variety of characters like 'Sir Gregory Goose' and 'Sir Tunbelly Clumsy', and they were supposed to keep these identities until midnight. Some Victorians, however, disliked these characters, which also appeared on cakes and on early Christmas 'scraps': they are 'either commonplace or gross' writes Hone; 'when genteel they are inane; when humorous, they are vulgar.'

Before long the cake itself became transferred to the Christmas Day table whilst the figures were replaced by that of Santa Claus with his attendant robins and reindeer. Twelfth-night parties became largely a thing of the past: only the ceremonial burning of holly and mistletoe and the dowsing of the great Yule Log remained to mark the ending of the Christmas season.

*Though clearly influenced by the 'Greenaway' fashion, these two cards
have their own distinctive charm.*

*A group of children are playing together in spring-time;
apparently their game is hide-and-seek for the message reads,
'May you find all the pleasures you seek for this SEASON.'
The card on which it is printed has been mounted on
a heavier, gilt-edged card.*

*Though nibbled at the corners, this folded invitation card has
survived for nearly a century. The brightly coloured figures
of the children are surrounded by a pale blue border with a spray
of ivy leaves. Inside a verse reads
'Now don't forget the day and hour,
But keep this card to tell,
And fix it on your looking-glass
Where you can see it well.'*

*'Dear Ernie', to whom the card is addressed, presumably enjoyed
the party and, fortunately, did not lose his invitation.*

INDEX

Acton, Eliza 8, 16, 20, 24, 26, 38, 42, 43, 48
Alderman in Chains (Turkey with sausages) 34
Almond paste (Marzipan) 40
Apple Florentine 44
    Hedgehog 44
    Yule Logs 44
Apples, Blazing 44
'Auld Man's Milk' 48

Bacon, stuffed chine of 8
Balmoral, recipes from 56
Bannock, Selkirk 52
    Yule 24
Bannocks, oatmeal 52
Bara Brith 50
Barley sugar 26
Beef, roast sirloin of 46
    Welsh spiced 46
'Bishop', Oxford recipe 48
    Mrs Dalgairns' 48
Black Bun (Hogmanay Bun) 50
Boar's Head, stuffed and decorated 30
    sauce for 30
Bonbons, chocolate 27
    Palace 26
Brawn 30

Caledonian cream 56
Candied flowers 26
Candy 26
Cassis 21
Chestnut sauce 34
    stuffing 34
Chicken patties 42
Chocolate almonds 27
    bonbons 26
    drops 27
Christmas cake (plum cake) 41
Christmas puddings, Ingoldsby 39
Christmas pye, Yorkshire 18
Christmas tourte à la Chatelaine 16
Cowslip wine 20
Crystallized fruit 26
Currant loaf, Yorkshire 10

Dalgairns, Mrs 24, 38, 48, 50, 52
Dods, Mrs Meg 14, 18, 21, 30, 32, 38, 48, 56, 61
Dolby, Richard 8, 12, 27, 55

'Egg-hot' 60
Elderberry wine 21
Englishwoman's Domestic Magazine, The 20, 28, 44

Flummery, oatmeal (Sowans) 12
    'a Temple in' 12
Frumenty, Durham 12
    Somerset 12

Galantine of fowl 43
Galette (shortbread) 34
Game: hare 58
    pheasant 59
    venison 56
Game soup 58
Ginger biscuits 28
    brandy 20–21

Gingerbread, Queen's 28
    men 28
Ginger nuts, rich sweetmeat 28
Ginger wine 20
Glasse, Mrs Hannah 18, 22, 32, 36, 40, 43, 46, 61
God-cakes, Coventry 22, 52
Goose giblet pie 18
Goose pye 18
Goose, roasted 32
    savoury sauce for 32
    stuffing 32
    with chestnuts 32
Gravy for turkey 34

Haggis, lamb's 54
    spiced 55
Ham, baked 8
    boiled 8
    home curing of 8
Ham in Marchpane 8
Hare, terrine of 58
Healthful Cookery Book, The 12, 28, 34, 38
'Het Pint' 48
Hunter's soup 58

Icing for a great cake 40

Kichel (God-cakes) 22, 52
Kichener, Dr 33, 34, 46

'Lamb's Wool' (Wassail Bowl) 60
Lent pies 15

MacIver, Mrs 18, 26, 32, 36, 50, 54
Marchpane (marzipan) 40
    ham in 8
Mincemeat, egg 15
    lemon 15
    to store 15
    with beef 14
    with tongue 15
    without meat 14
Mince pies, glazed 16
    puff paste for 16
    royal 16
Mulled drinks 48
Mushroom catsup 33
Mutton pies, with rum 55

New Year cakes 52
Nougat 26–7

Party dishes 42–3
    menu for 1850 43
Peacock 32
Petticoat tails (shortbread) 24
Pheasant, stewed with cabbage 59
Pies, raised 18
    hot-water paste for 18
    puff paste for 16
Pig's face, stuffed 30
Pig's head, in imitation of wild boar 30
Plum cakes, marzipan for 40
    rich 40
    to ice 40
    with yeast 40

Plum pudding, a small very rich 38
    a superfine 38
    sauces for 38
Plumb pudding 36
Plumb porridge, English, Scottish to make for
    Christmas, for Lent pottage 36
Pork pie, Cheshire 43
Posset, sack 61
    'wassail-bowl' for eating 61
Powell's Family Companion 34
Punch 48

Queen Victoria soup 56

Roasting, art of 34
    beef 46
    turkey 34
    venison 56
Rundell, Mrs 8, 12, 14, 15, 18, 58

Sauce, Dr Hunter's 33
    for plum pudding 38
    for turkey 34
    Robert 33
Shoesmith, Thomas 16, 28
Shortbread (yule bannock), Ayrshire 24
    plain 24
    rich 24
Shrub, lemon 20
    orange 20
Snow cream 44
    pudding 44
Sowans (flummery) 12
Soyer, Alexis 8, 30, 32, 34, 43, 59
Spice cakes, Yorkshire 11
'Star' Book of Prize Recipes 11, 26, 29

Tourte, puff paste for 16
    Christmas, à la Chatelaine 16
Turkey, roasted 34
    stuffed with chestnuts 34
    with oysters 34
    with sausages (Alderman in Chains) 34
Turkey stuffing 34
Twelfth Night cake, customs 62
    decorations for 62
    Dr Kichener's 62
    Thomas Shoesmith's 62

Venison, hashed from Balmoral 56
    roasted 56

Wassail Bowl (Lamb's Wool) 60
    'a centre supper-dish' 61
Wigs 22–3
Wines and liqueurs, to make 20–21
    mulled 48

Yorkshire pudding 46
Yule loaf, from Cornwall 11
    Scotland 10–11
    Yorkshire 10
    to keep fresh 11